A GUIDE TO USING CORPORA FOR ENGLISH LANGUAGE LEARNERS

D0165244

A GUIDE TO USING CORPORA FOR ENGLISH LANGUAGE LEARNERS

Empowering language learners to become independent learners through corpus-aided discovery and investigation

Robert Poole

EDINBURGH
University Press

Edinburgh University Press is one of the leading university presses in the UK. We publish academic books and journals in our selected subject areas across the humanities and social sciences, combining cutting-edge scholarship with high editorial and production values to produce academic works of lasting importance. For more information visit our website: edinburghuniversitypress.com

© Robert Poole, 2018

Edinburgh University Press Ltd
The Tun – Holyrood Road, 12(2f) Jackson's Entry, Edinburgh EH8 8PJ

Typeset in Baskerville MT Pro by Biblichor Ltd, and
printed and bound in Great Britain.

A CIP record for this book is available from the British Library

ISBN 978 1 4744 2716 6 (hardback)
ISBN 978 1 4744 2718 0 (webready PDF)
ISBN 978 1 4744 2717 3 (paperback)
ISBN 978 1 4744 2719 7 (epub)

The right of Robert Poole to be identified as the author of this work has been asserted in accordance with the Copyright, Designs and Patents Act 1988, and the Copyright and Related Rights Regulations 2003 (SI No. 2498).

CONTENTS

TO LANGUAGE LEARNERS

IF YOU ARE choosing this book to continue your language studies, you may be familiar with and understand the potential of using a corpus for developing your language ability. As you may know, a **corpus** (plural: **corpora**) is a large collection of authentic language which has been collected for a variety of purposes. Researchers use corpora to study language use and language change over time, lexicographers and textbook writers use corpora to develop resources and learning materials, and language learners use corpora to explore language and answer their own questions about language use. You may still be asking, 'But why do these groups choose to use corpora instead of other resources?' There are several answers to this question. First, as stated in its definition, a corpus is a collection of *authentic* language. These are not examples imagined and created to highlight a particular word or part of speech. These are sentences spoken and written by real language users in real world situations and contexts. If researchers, teachers, and learners are going to study and explore language in order to better understand how it is used, it seems only reasonable that we should look at the actual language people use rather than imaginary examples.

Second, corpora are used to study language because often what people believe about how, when, or why they use a particular word or phrase is often inaccurate or even incorrect. It's simply true that most people rarely consider questions such as 'What is the difference between near-synonyms like *hear* and *listen* or *beautiful* and *attractive*?' or reflect on the differences between *when* and *while*. Thus, it is only natural that people may not give accurate answers to these questions. So, for researchers, instructors, and learners, it can be more useful to search a corpus for data rather trusting our own or another person's intuition about language use.

Third, and related to the prior reason, corpora can help you become an independent and autonomous language learner. Rather than waiting to ask a question to a classmate or instructor, you will be able to ask and answer your own questions. Through this process of discovery, your language skills will develop as you carefully read and think about the information you are presented, and you will be able to make informed decisions about language choices.

This text provides a step-by-step, hands-on approach to help you advance your own language ability. As you move through the text, take time to reflect on the findings and complete your own corpus searches.

To the corpus!

KEY FEATURES

- Step-by-step illustrated examples to help readers achieve the potential of corpus linguistics for language learning
- Tutorials using a variety of popular corpora
- Opportunities for additional reflection and practice throughout the text
- Tutorials aimed at promoting learner autonomy and self-discovery

TO LANGUAGE TEACHERS

THIS BOOK IS also directed to graduate students in TESOL and applied linguistics as well as language teachers who may wish to learn more about how to implement corpus activities in the classroom. I have often spoken with graduate students and language teachers who have said, 'I'm interested in doing corpus activities, but I'm not sure how,' or, 'I want to do corpus activities in my class, but I don't have time.' This book has emerged from these very statements. As a composition teacher in a first-year writing programme, I understand the challenge of balancing attention to rhetoric, process, and documentation while also trying to address the language needs of second language learners. The activities in this text attempt to find a happy medium between these various concerns. Many of the tutorials in this book were developed in response to particular classroom realities such as a need to develop my students' abilities to revise papers or improve word choice. Thus, the activities were initially created to solve particular needs of my students. Rather than consistently commenting on essays 'Avoid this . . .' or 'You should do that . . .', I have developed a number of targeted corpus searches for students. These searches are designed to produce 'Aha!' moments that will help students make more effective choices in their own writing.

In this text, you will learn how to help students complete searches to revise their essays, create wordlists for vocabulary study, investigate collocates to improve word choice, and see how corpus searches can stimulate engaging classroom conversation and even facilitate student research projects. Throughout the text, there are sections titled 'Your Turn' that ask readers to pursue their own searches and reach their own conclusions about language use.

I hope those earlier stated concerns of 'How?' and 'When?' will be mitigated as the tutorials help you see how you can design your own activities and the learning outcomes that may be achieved while also providing you with classroom-ready activities that you can begin implementing in your classrooms immediately.

INTRODUCTION

IF YOU WERE to ask a group of native English speakers to list the three most common adjectives that are used to describe the noun *fisherman*, it is highly probable that many would list the adjective *avid*. Despite having countless adjectives from which to choose, the native speaker is much more likely to list *avid* than other seemingly appropriate adjectives such as *skilled*, *enthusiastic*, *passionate*, or *zealous*. In **corpus linguistics**, *avid* is considered a **collocate** of *fisherman* because the two co-occur with great frequency. If you ask the same question regarding *fisherman* and adjectives of English language learners, it is equally unlikely that many would write *avid* on their list. Since *avid* is not an especially common adjective, it is certainly possible that a language learner has never encountered the word. This type of collocational knowledge is possessed by native speakers who have years of experience in the language but is not as easily acquired by learners. Importantly, this example of words preferring particular partners is not an anomaly; it is a common occurrence in language.

So, what is a corpus? A corpus is simply a large collection of authentic language collected from newspapers, blogs, academic essays, and so on that has been compiled, organised, and made searchable. For example, there are corpora of student essays, political speeches, academic lectures, newspaper articles, blogs, and much more. By collecting and analysing real language from real contexts, we can learn a great deal about language and how it is used. Corpus study has shown repeatedly that words often appear together in chunks and bundles and often display a preference for each other. For example, native speakers implicitly know that *strong coffee* is preferred instead of *powerful coffee*. Another example to highlight the importance of collocational knowledge for language users are the synonyms *attractive* and *beautiful*. The dictionary definitions of these words would indicate that these items could be essentially interchangeable in speaking and writing. However, these words occur in rather distinct contexts.

Think about it!

Think for a moment about which nouns these two adjectives, *attractive* and *beautiful*, are most often used to modify. Make a list of five nouns you believe each of these two adjectives commonly modifies.

beautiful + noun

1. _____
2. _____
3. _____
4. _____
5. _____

attractive + noun

1. _____
2. _____
3. _____
4. _____
5. _____

A quick search of the 560 million word Corpus of Contemporary American English (COCA) (https://corpus.byu.edu) reveals that *day, mind, eyes, song,* and *piece* are most often modified by *beautiful,* but the nouns *alternative, option, candidate, investment,* and *prices* are common collocates of the adjective *attractive* (see the chart below). Thus, while native English speakers produce language that generally follows these patterns, we must again consider how an ESL/EFL learner can gain this knowledge and the effects on accuracy and comprehensibility a lack of collocational knowledge has for the language learner. You may think that it is of little consequence whether a learner utters *beautiful candidate* rather than *attractive candidate*. However, this structure, *beautiful candidate*, could lead to pauses in the conversation or lack of understanding, or could even cause the listener to be offended. Imagine then if such non-standard collocations appeared regularly in the utterances of a language learner.

Collocates of *beautiful* and *attractive*

	WORD 1 (W1): BEAUTIFUL (3.85)	W1	W2	W1/W2	SCORE		WORD 2 (W2): ATTRACTIVE (0.26)	W2	W1	W2/W1	SCORE
1	DAY	576	0	1,152.0	299.0	1	ALTERNATIVE	118	0	236.0	909.1
2	MIND	210	0	420.0	109.0	2	OPTION	135	1	135.0	520.1
3	EYES	184	0	368.0	95.5	3	CANDIDATE	47	0	94.0	362.1
4	SONG	141	0	282.0	73.2	4	INVESTMENT	31	0	62.0	238.8
5	NIGHT	102	0	204.0	53.0	5	FORCE	29	0	58.0	223.4
6	SPRING	83	0	166.0	43.1	6	PRICES	29	0	58.0	223.4
7	HERE	82	0	164.0	42.6	7	PROPOSITION	22	0	44.0	169.5
8	MUSIC	161	1	161.0	41.8	8	OFFER	20	0	40.0	154.1
9	COUNTRY	151	1	151.0	39.2	9	ALTERNATIVES	19	0	38.0	146.4
10	PIECE	115	1	115.0	29.9	10	NUISANCE	18	0	36.0	138.7
11	SOUND	55	0	110.0	28.6	11	TARGETS	33	1	33.0	127.1
12	HAIR	100	1	100.0	26.0	12	PRICE	27	1	27.0	104.0
13	WEDDING	50	0	100.0	26.0	13	DEFENDANTS	12	0	24.0	92.5
14	GARDENS	48	0	96.0	24.9	14	RETURNS	12	0	24.0	92.5
15	CITY	191	2	95.5	24.8	15	DESTINATION	20	1	20.0	77.0

Collocational knowledge, that is, knowing to say *beautiful eyes* but not *beautiful prices*, is only one of the many benefits corpus study can bring to your language learning classroom or your personal language study. Understanding how to use corpora as a resource, learners can balance their intuition with knowledge gained from viewing authentic samples of language and can make language choices that are grounded in actual language use rather than invented and inauthentic examples. Further, you can become an independent learner as you investigate language and explore grammatical patterns, do searches to help revise an essay, or learn about differences in language use between different contexts and genres. In this book, you will learn how to perform corpus searches, how to use corpus searches to guide language decisions, and even how to build your own specialised corpus that will help you learn about the language style of your academic or professional area of interest.

Organisation of the book

Each chapter contains corpus searches designed to help you gain the skills necessary to complete language searches and reach conclusions about language. The step-by-step instructions for each search are included in addition to illustrations that help guide you through the fundamentals of corpus linguistics. As you progress through the book, you will be prompted to complete your own searches and analyse your own findings. Remember, one of the great benefits of corpus study is developing independence as a language learner by asking and answering your own questions about language. I hope this book will give you the skills to investigate language on your own. So, please use the searches here as a platform for solving your own language challenges.

Corpus notes

All of the corpora used in this book are free and available through the internet. The collection of corpora at https://corpus.byu.edu that is used frequently in the tutorials asks users to register and create a free account. To register, users simply need to provide their name and email address, create a password, click whether they are a teacher or student, and agree to terms and conditions. As a registered student user, you are able to conduct 50 free searches per day; language teachers receive 100 free searches per day. If you do not register, you will be able to do 20 searches per day.

For a full list of corpora and corpus tools used in the book along with other corpus tools and resources you may wish to explore, see 'Corpus Resources' following Chapter 5.

To the corpus!

1 LEARNING THE ESSENTIALS

THE FIRST SEARCHES are designed to introduce you to the basic search functions of the Corpus of Contemporary American English (COCA), the British National Corpus (BNC), and the Global Web-based English Corpus (GloWbE). While these are the main corpora used in this textbook and perhaps the most widely used corpora in the world, there are many corpora and corpus resources available online for you to use. In fact, on the same website we will use to access the COCA and BNC, you can also search the Time Magazine Corpus, the Wikipedia Corpus, the Strathy Corpus of Canadian English, and several others. We will use many corpora for the searches in this text, but you can also find a list and descriptions of other corpus resources following Chapter 5. Importantly, the knowledge of basic searches you learn in this chapter and in this book can be transferred to most available corpora. In other words, the way you do searches in the COCA and BNC is the same way you do searches in other places too.

First, go to https://corpus.byu.edu. On the homepage, you can see the list of available corpora. Before clicking on one of the corpora, click the *Register* link on the drop-down list under *my account*, and complete the free and quick registration process. With your student account, you will be able to conduct 50 free searches per day. After you register, click on the COCA. Let's get started!

corpus.byu.edu

corpora, size, queries = better resources, more insight

Created by Mark Davies, BYU. Overview, search types, looking at variation, corpus-based resources, updates.

The most widely used online corpora -- more than 130,000 distinct researchers, teachers, and students each month.

English	# words	language/dialect	time period	compare
NOW Corpus NEW	2.8 billion+	20 countries / Web	2010-yesterday	
Global Web-Based English (GloWbE)	1.9 billion	20 countries / Web	2012-13	
Wikipedia Corpus	1.9 billion	English	-2014	Info
Hansard Corpus (British Parliament)	1.6 billion	British	1803-2005	Info
Corpus of Contemporary American English (COCA)	520 million	American	1990-2015	★ ★ ★ ★ ★
Corpus of Historical American English (COHA)	400 million	American	1810-2009	★ ★
TIME Magazine Corpus	100 million	American	1923-2006	
Corpus of American Soap Operas	100 million	American	2001-2012	★
British National Corpus (BYU-BNC)*	100 million	British	1980s-1993	★ ★
Strathy Corpus (Canada)	50 million	Canadian	1970s-2000s	
CORE Corpus NEW	50 million	Web registers	-2014	
Other languages				
Corpus del Español (see also...)	100 million	Spanish	1200s-1900s	★
Corpus do Português (see also...)	45 million	Portuguese	1300s-1900s	
N-grams				
Google Books: American English	155 billion	American	1500s-2000s	★
Google Books: British English	34 billion	British	1500s-2000s	
Google Books: One Million Books	89 billion	Am/Br	1500s-2000s	
Google Books: Spanish	45 billion	Spanish	1500s-2000s	

Search 1: Awesome!

At the top left of the screen, you will see five options: (1) List, (2) Chart, (3) Collocates, (4) Compare, and (5) KWIC. As the chapter and the book continue, we will discuss each of these search options. However, for our first search, let's do the simplest and most basic search possible: a word search using the *List* function.

Step 1: Click the *List* button in the upper left side of the interface

List	Chart Collocates Compare KWIC
	[POS]
Find matching strings	Reset
Sections Texts/Virtual Sort/Limit Options	

Step 2: In the search box, type the adjective *awesome*

List	Chart Collocates Compare KWIC
awesome	[POS]
Find matching strings	Reset
Sections Texts/Virtual Sort/Limit Options	

Step 3: Click *Find matching strings*

		CONTEXT	FREQ
1		AWESOME	5561

As you will see in the results, the *List* search only provides the number of times, approximately 5,500 times, the word occurs in the corpus. This basic frequency information will probably not be enough to answer many of the questions you'll hope to answer through using the corpus. However, if you click on the word *awesome* in the results window, you will be able to see sample sentences that use the word. These sample sentences are called **concordance lines**. Reading, analysing, and discussing concordance lines can be a useful vocabulary learning activity because these lines are authentic samples of the word in which you are interested. If you had never noticed the word *awesome* before doing the search, the concordance lines give you access to literally thousands of sentences using the word.

Step 4: Click *awesome*

15	2015	MAG	GolfMag	A	B	C	. A couple of bogeys down the stretch on Sunday, but otherwise it was awesome to watch. # You also had some good early showings at Augusta, with
16	2015	MAG	GolfMag	A	B	C	, " You won! " He was genuinely excited for me, which is awesome. That's a rare thing in pro golf. He's such a good
17	2015	MAG	MilitaryHist	A	B	C	emplacements in the woods near Crpy. # TABLE # Though the Paris Guns were an awesome technological achievement they had no impact on the outcome of W
18	2015	MAG	MotherJones	A	B	C	, changing food names, and adding a toppings station. " It's so awesome to see a student who went over to the salad bar to put some cumin
19	2015	MAG	MotherJones	A	B	C	generally inclined to give themselves more credit. So their calibration was' I'm awesome; this is super easy,' when I felt like I was doing poorly
20	2015	MAG	MotherJones	A	B	C	unravel the secrets of the place. The plot (which my 1o-year-old declared " awesome ") is a clever ploy to impart coding fundamentals, as inspired by that
21	2015	MAG	NatlReview	A	B	C	" (whatever the hell those are), and to take in the " awesome, dude " vibe of it all within sight of cattle and bales of hayit
22	2015	NEWS	WashPost	A	B	C	as terse chief executive and a sometimes flippant writer who sprinkled his messages with " awesome, " " my bad " and " chill out. " Bush has cast
23	2015	NEWS	WashPost	A	B	C	. so they know what people had to go through to make it such an awesome community, such a progressive community. " But how critical are architectural details
24	2015	NEWS	WashPost	A	B	C	of 51,176 in Montreal, Ellis said: " Oh, man, it was awesome. " She and the players will enjoy massive support again Sunday. With fans
25	2015	NEWS	WashPost	A	B	C	zone; and the difference between talent and hard-earned experience. " David is an awesome talent, and a lot of players make it to the league on pure talent

While viewing the concordance lines, you can click on any of the sentences to see more of the sample. The concordance lines only give us a piece of the sentence, but if you click on the name of the source in the fourth column on the left side of the screen, you can get a larger piece of the source text.

Step 5: Click for more context

Date	2015
Publication information	Apr2015, Vol. 57 Issue 4, p104-108. 5p. 4 Color Photographs.
Title	CRAIG STADLER The Walrus in Winter
Author	Sens, Josh;
Source	MAG: Golf Magazine

Expanded context:

There's an embarrassment factor for you? Do you really think Masters fans care what you shoot? # Well, I have no interest in being part of anything where I shoot 81, 80. # When did Augusta start to get too difficult for you? # For five years or so, I'd been saying under my breath to friends that the first year Kevin got in was going to be my last. And it worked out perfectly, because he played really well. A couple of bogeys down the stretch on Sunday, but otherwise it was awesome to watch. # You also had some good early showings at Augusta, with a win and three top-10 finishes in your first nine starts. # A lot of it came down to putting. I always seemed to putt well there, but I don't know why. # In 1982, the year you won, you had a three-shot lead going into Sunday. What does it feel like to sleep on the 54-hole Masters lead? # A bunch of us were right up there on Saturday,

Search 2: Where does *awesome* occur?

As you saw with search 1, the *List* search option provides basic information about the number of times a word is used by speakers and writers. The second search option is *Chart*. This search option creates results in a bar chart format to display how many times a word is used in spoken, fiction, newspaper, magazine, and academic **registers**. This search is great for comparing how a word is used in different contexts and can help you decide whether a word is formal or informal. For example, if a word is commonly used in the spoken but not in the academic register, you can likely assume that the word is informal. Let's try a search and see what we discover.

Step 1: Click the *Chart* button

Step 2: Enter *awesome* in the search box

List | Chart | Collocates Compare KWIC

awesome   [POS]

See frequency by section | Reset

Step 3: Click *see frequency by section* to complete the search

SECTION (CLICK FOR SUB-SECTIONS) (SEE ALL SECTIONS AT ONCE)	FREQ	SIZE (M)	PER MIL	CLICK FOR CONTEXT (SEE ALL)
SPOKEN	1850	109.4	16.91	
FICTION	779	104.9	7.43	
MAGAZINE	1496	110.1	13.59	
NEWSPAPER	1090	106.0	10.29	
ACADEMIC	341	103.4	3.30	
1990-1994	624	104.0	6.00	
1995-1999	749	103.4	7.24	
2000-2004	834	102.9	8.10	
2005-2009	1191	102.0	11.67	
2010-2015	2158	121.6	17.75	

After clicking *see frequency by section*, you will see the bar chart results. You will see how *awesome* is used in different contexts and how its frequency of usage has changed over time. Observe also that the results show you **frequency**, the number of times a word is used, and the **per million rate**, the number of times the word is used every 1 million words in that section of the corpus.

Well, what do you notice? Where is the word used most frequently? Where is it rarely used? Does this mean the word is more formal or informal? We can clearly see that *awesome* is used most commonly in spoken English, but it is rarely used in the academic register. This indicates that it would be best to use this word to describe a movie to your friends or describe your latte at Starbucks but would not be appropriate to describe a theory or explain a historical event in an academic presentation or essay. This type of search can help you make decisions about where to use a word and where you probably should not use the word.

YOUR TURN 1.1

Imagine you are trying to decide whether a word is informal or formal and appropriate to use in an essay you are writing. A quick corpus search can help us make this decision. Perform a *Chart* search for the word *however*.

1. Where (for example, spoken, fiction, magazine, newspaper, academic) is the word most often used?

   _____

2. Where is it rarely used?

   _____

3. What guideline could we create to help guide our language use?

   _____

   _____

   _____

Tip: Click Chart *and enter* however *in the search box. Also, click on any of the bars in the chart to see sample sentences of the word. This can help you see how to punctuate or include a word in your writing.*

YOUR TURN 1.2

Think of a word you have recently encountered. Perhaps you heard someone use it at a coffee shop or a teacher used it in class. Search for the word
using the *Chart* option.

Word: _____

1. Where (for example, spoken, fiction, magazine, newspaper, academic) is
   the word most frequently used?

   _____

2. From reading a few concordance lines, what do you think the word
   means?

   _____

   _____

   _____

Search 3: What words are often used with *awesome*?

The third search function in the corpus allows us to search for collocates of *awesome*. If you recall from the Introduction, collocates are words which often appear together. In fact, if one word occurs, we can expect that the other word will also occur. For example, native speakers use the collocate *strong coffee* but rarely use the expression *powerful coffee*. Thus, *strong* and *coffee* are collocates because they appear together rather frequently. It can be quite helpful when learning a new word to see the other words, that is, the collocates, which are used regularly with our word of interest. In this search, we will identify which words are often used together with *awesome*.

Step 1: Click *Collocates* on the search page

Step 2: Enter *awesome* in the search bar

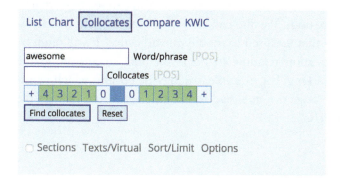

Notice the numbers 4, 3, 2, 1 . . . below the search bar. This is called the **collocation window**. When this is set at 4 to the left and 4 to the right as it is now, we will get results that show us the most common words used within the 4L–4R window of *awesome*.

Step 3: Click *Find collocates*

		CONTEXT	FREQ
1	☐	!	328
2	☐	POWER	163
3	☐	AWESOME	151
4	☐	PRETTY	101
5	☐	RESPONSIBILITY	93
6	☐	TOTALLY	62
7	☐	SIGHT	44
8	☐	TRULY	33
9	☐	TASK	31
10	☐	BEAUTY	21
11	☐	WOW	19
12	☐	DUDE	18
13	☐	DISPLAY	18
14	☐	TALENT	16
15	☐	POWERS	15

The list shows the top 15 words that occur with *awesome*. You can see that *awesome* is most often used in exclamations. We also can observe the nouns with which it is often used and the adverbs that are used to modify the adjective. It will often be useful to narrow the collocation window to help you find an answer to the language question you are asking. For example, we may be curious which words most commonly follow the adjective *awesome*. To do this, you could change the collocation window to 0L–1R.

Step 4: Click *Collocates*

Step 5: Change the collocation window to 0L–1R

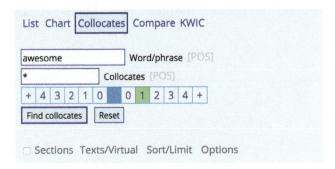

Step 6: Click *Find collocates*

		CONTEXT	FREQ
1	☐	!	191
2	☐	POWER	115
3	☐	RESPONSIBILITY	81
4	☐	SIGHT	41
5	☐	THING	36
6	☐	JOB	30
7	☐	TASK	28
8	☐	EXPERIENCE	27
9	☐	FEELING	23
10	☐	GOD	20
11	☐	GUY	16
12	☐	FORCE	15
13	☐	BEAUTY	14
14	☐	DISPLAY	13
15	☐	OPPORTUNITY	12

Now, instead of seeing all of the words which occur in the 4L–4R window, we see only the words that often appear after *awesome*. We will see later how to use part-of-speech searches to help us narrow results even further, but this search is still quite helpful.

YOUR TURN 1.3

Think of a word you have encountered recently in a textbook (for example, *research, consist, dynamic, theory*) or in a classroom discussion. Before searching for your word, think of 5 collocates that you think will likely appear frequently with the word.

Word: _____

Likely collocates:

1._____ 2._____ 3._____ 4._____ 5._____

Do a collocates search.

1. Which words most frequently appear with your word?

_____

2. Was your original list similar to the corpus results?

_____

3. Which results were surprising?

_____
_____
_____

Search 4: Are *beautiful* and *attractive* interchangeable?

The next search function is called *Compare*. As you've probably guessed, this function allows you to compare how two words are used. Many times as a language learner you will likely feel unsure of which word to choose in a particular situation. You may ask, 'What's the difference between major and main?' or, 'When do I use listen or hear?' and so on. Using this function can give us some evidence that will help us make this choice. For this search, we'll use some adjectives other than *awesome*. We saw in the Introduction the differences in usage of *beautiful* and *attractive*, but let's now go through the steps of how these findings were reached.

Step 1: Click *Compare*

Step 2: Enter *beautiful* in one search box and *attractive* in the next

Step 3: Change the collocation window to 0L–1R

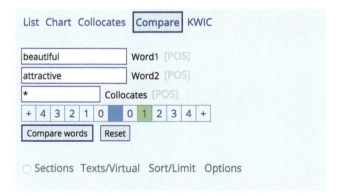

Step 4: Click *Compare words*

WORD 1 (W1): BEAUTIFUL (3.85)							WORD 2 (W2): ATTRACTIVE (0.26)					
	WORD	W1	W2	W1/W2	SCORE			WORD	W2	W1	W2/W1	SCORE
1	DAY	576	0	1,152.0	299.0		1	ALTERNATIVE	118	0	236.0	909.1
2	MIND	210	0	420.0	109.0		2	OPTION	135	1	135.0	520.1
3	EYES	184	0	368.0	95.5		3	CANDIDATE	47	0	94.0	362.1
4	SONG	141	0	282.0	73.2		4	INVESTMENT	31	0	62.0	238.8
5	NIGHT	102	0	204.0	53.0		5	FORCE	29	0	58.0	223.4
6	SPRING	83	0	166.0	43.1		6	PRICES	29	0	58.0	223.4
7	HERE	82	0	164.0	42.6		7	PROPOSITION	22	0	44.0	169.5
8	MUSIC	161	1	161.0	41.8		8	OFFER	20	0	40.0	154.1
9	COUNTRY	151	1	151.0	39.2		9	ALTERNATIVES	19	0	38.0	146.4
10	PIECE	115	1	115.0	29.9		10	NUISANCE	18	0	36.0	138.7
11	SOUND	55	0	110.0	28.6		11	TARGETS	33	1	33.0	127.1
12	HAIR	100	1	100.0	26.0		12	PRICE	27	1	27.0	104.0
13	WEDDING	50	0	100.0	26.0		13	DEFENDANTS	12	0	24.0	92.5
14	GARDENS	48	0	96.0	24.9		14	RETURNS	12	0	24.0	92.5
15	CITY	191	2	95.5	24.8		15	DESTINATION	20	1	20.0	77.0

It's rather stunning just how differently the words are used. While we may think of these two words as almost exact synonyms, they are actually used to describe different types of nouns. Again, learning the common collocates can help you with fluency and comprehension.

YOUR TURN 1.4

Two words that English language learners may often confuse are *when* and *while*. Yes, most grammar books do give a rule for learners to follow, but it can be more useful to analyse data and create your own rule. Using the *Compare* search function, identify a pattern in how the two words are used and create a guideline to follow in your own language use.

Pattern: _____

Guideline:

_____

_____

_____

Tip: In the collocation window, enter 0 for the left and 4 for the right. This is because we are more interested in the words which appear after when *and* while *than before.*

Hint: *Which tense are the verbs following* when *and* while?

YOUR TURN 1.5

Think of two more words that are quite similar in meaning. Before you search for the words, make a list of the collocates you think will appear with your words.

Word 1 + collocates:

_____ + 1) _____ 2) _____ 3) _____ 4) _____

Word 2 + collocates:

_____ + 1) _____ 2) _____ 3) _____ 4) _____

Now, use the *Compare* search to find results on the two words (*remember to narrow the numbers in the collocates boxes to help you focus on the results*).

1. Which collocates regularly appear with your two words?

   _____

2. Are the words in the corpus results the same as the words on your personal list?

   _____

3. Make a guideline on how to use the two words.

   _____

   _____

   _____

Search 5: Grammatical patterns with *awesome*

Each search function allows us to see language from a different angle and often makes possible fresh insights about a word and how it is used. As you saw with the *List* search function, we only get to see the frequency of how many times a word appears in the corpus while the second function, *Chart*, allows us to view how a word is used in different contexts. The next function, *Keyword in Context (KWIC)* shows the search term in sentences with the words around it colour-coded for parts of speech (abbreviated POS in the corpus). This function makes it possible for us to visualise the grammatical patterns in which a word appears. So, let's experiment with the *KWIC* function.

Step 1: Click the *KWIC* button

Step 2: Enter *awesome* in the search box

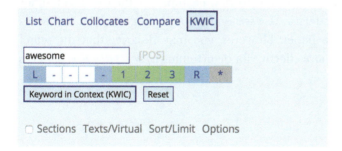

Step 3: Click *Keyword in Context (KWIC)*

5	1996	NEWS	Denver	A B C	championship courses . The Canyon Course winds through the	awesome	beauty of Esperrero Canyon and includes the lunar-like rock
6	2015	NEWS	Austin	A B C	Awesome show Max Gregor : (Tim and Eric) were	awesome	but also kind of a disaster . There was a box of
7	2010	MAG	Essence	A B C	the image of a Black mother running the White House is	awesome	but also natural . We prepared Elenni and her peers for this
8	1994	FIC	MassachRev	A B C	contemporary masters .) They will continue to display an	awesome	capacity for this sort of contempt well into the future , to
9	2011	SPOK	NBC_Today	A B C	and prescription sunglasses . GIFFORD: They 're an awesome ,	awesome	company	KOTB: So you buy one , one goes to help
10	2008	FIC	Bk:FiancéAtHerFingertips	A B C	was without funds , period . // " But I have	awesome	credit	she 'd assured him . // " Yes ?
11	2002	NEWS	Houston	A B C	setter , and they are strong all around . We played	awesome	defense and really dug everything . There were some very long
12	2003	NEWS	Atlanta	A B C	east , with sailboats plying Puget Sound and Mount Rainier 's	awesome	dome in the background . # Now that 's a civic welcome
13	1999	FIC	Analog	A B C	of the matter was that what I was experiencing was too	awesome	ever to be captured by Vreality or any other medium . The
14	1993	MAG	AmerArtist	A B C	greatest amount of atmosphere . During daylight , there 's an	awesome	feeling of space and distance created by the loss of yellow that
15	2005	MAG	OutdoorLife	A B C	on Nantucket Island EAST : SCOUTING REPORT 141 ADVENTURE Find	awesome	fishing on the remote , 740-mile Northern Forest Canoe Trail 142

Tip: There is a key for the colour codes on the COCA website when you click '?' at the top of the screen. Also, notice that the results are ordered alphabetically by the word which appears following our search term. Use the 're-sort' option above the results to change how the lines are ordered.

The colour-coded *KWIC* lines are an excellent way to visualise the patterns in which a word appears. With *awesome*, we can see it regularly occurs in an *article + awesome + noun* pattern. Using *KWIC* searches can be useful for determining the proper preposition to use following a noun. For example, if you do a *KWIC* search with the word *experience*, you will be able to view examples of the word with different *experience + preposition* patterns. As a writer, this can be an excellent tool to use when writing or revising a paper. However, you may discover that the search process in search 7 is even more effective for determining *noun + preposition* patterns.

Search 6: Which words are synonyms of *awesome*?

We have now performed searches using the five main functions of the corpus, but there are more ways we can narrow our results to help us answer specific language questions. Another search option we can use is a synonym search. We have already seen that *awesome* is not used frequently within academic writing and speaking, so maybe we can use a corpus search to find a more appropriate word for our situation.

Step 1: Click *List*

Step 2: Enter *=awesome* in the search bar and click *Find matching strings*

List	Chart Collocates Compare KWIC

=awesome   [POS]

Find matching strings   Reset

☐ Sections Texts/Virtual Sort/Limit Options

Step 3: View search results

		CONTEXT	FREQ
1	☐	GRAND [S]	37993
2	☐	AMAZING [S]	26293
3	☐	REMARKABLE [S]	16141
4	☐	TREMENDOUS [S]	15154
5	☐	OVERWHELMING [S]	10816
6	☐	AWESOME [S]	6504
7	☐	SPLENDID [S]	2961
8	☐	ASTOUNDING [S]	2085
9	☐	BREATHTAKING [S]	1926
10	☐	FEARSOME [S]	987
11	☐	HUMBLING [S]	756
12	☐	AWE-INSPIRING [S]	389

Step 4: Click on the word *amazing* to view concordance lines

CLICK FOR MORE CONTEXT				[?]	SAVE LIST	CHOOSE LIST	————	CREATE NEW LIST		[?]	
1	2015	NEWS	WashPost	A B C	. " I am so very thankful to God and His Son Jesus for the amazing talented group of' apostles' He chose to work at my side as we
2	2015	NEWS	WashPost	A B C	commander of all U.S. military forces in the Middle East. " We agreed how amazing it must be that you're single-handedly re-writing history, " she added, recallir
3	2015	NEWS	WashPost	A B C	it the second most-watched show of the week after the Israeli version of " The Amazing Race. " The episode began with a spoof of the Israeli leaders as characte
4	2015	NEWS	WashPost	A B C	in the NCAA tournament's Final Four. And yet this may be the most amazing thing the Terps did this season: They voluntarily forfeited their cellphones for more
5	2015	NEWS	WashPost	A B C	system is broken. While he recognizes that what the entrepreneurs are doing is " amazing, " he said in an interview that their work is limited and a supplement
6	2015	NEWS	WashPost	A B C	actually be here in this gorgeous stadium and to be a part of it is amazing, " Camillo said. Growing up, Camillo - then known by her maiden
7	2015	NEWS	WashPost	A B C	given that he, um, doesn't exactly beat them out, that's amazing. Rodriguez is included here in part to acknowledge the " exhibition " portion of
10	2015	NEWS	WashPost (2)	A B C	in 2008 before 40,000 people in Nationals Park. " It was just an amazing experience, " she said. " What I teach my kids is it's

Step 5: Search *amazing* with *Chart* to see where it is used often

List Chart Collocates Compare KWIC

amazing   [POS]
See frequency by section   Reset

☐ Sections Texts/Virtual Sort/Limit Options

Step 6: Click *See frequency by section*

SECTION (CLICK FOR SUB-SECTIONS) (SEE ALL SECTIONS AT ONCE)	FREQ	SIZE (M)	PER MIL	CLICK FOR CONTEXT (SEE ALL)
SPOKEN	10704	109.4	97.85	
FICTION	3213	104.9	30.63	
MAGAZINE	4957	110.1	45.02	
NEWSPAPER	3810	106.0	35.96	
ACADEMIC	940	103.4	9.09	

Step 7: Search *remarkable* with *Chart* to see where it is used often

SECTION (CLICK FOR SUB-SECTIONS) (SEE ALL SECTIONS AT ONCE)	FREQ	SIZE (M)	PER MIL	CLICK FOR CONTEXT (SEE ALL)
SPOKEN	3772	109.4	34.48	
FICTION	1505	104.9	14.35	
MAGAZINE	3839	110.1	34.86	
NEWSPAPER	2790	106.0	26.33	
ACADEMIC	3134	103.4	30.30	

These results teach us something very important about using corpora: we have to investigate and explore to reach conclusions because the corpus does not simply give us the answer. Also, our corpus searches can give us information that may help guide our language use, but we still must consider our situation and make our own decisions. In the synonym search, we were able to find a list of synonyms of our search term *awesome*. However, the first item *grand* did not match what we were wanting. *Amazing* and *remarkable* were more similar, and our additional searches showed us that *remarkable* is used more often than the others in academic writing, but it still is not used much. Our lesson, thus, could be that we should avoid such strong adjectives in academic settings.

 YOUR TURN 1.6

Varying your word choice to avoid repetition is an important skill for academic writing. Think of an academic vocabulary word (for example, *consist, state, discover*) and complete a synonym search.

Word: _____

Top 5 synonyms:

1)_____ 2)_____ 3)_____ 4)_____ 5)_____

Search 7: Do I say *awesome at* or *awesome in*?

Another powerful search option we have is called a part-of-speech search, abbreviated as POS in the corpus. Using the POS search option can again help us narrow our findings so that we may focus on results towards our specific question. One question language learners often have is which prepositions to use with a particular word. For example, if I am writing a letter of application, would I write *experience in* or *experience on*? As we saw with search 6, the corpus does not always give us a clear and simple answer, but it does help us find examples that can assist us in reaching our own conclusions.

Step 1: Click *List* and enter *awesome* in the search bar

Step 2: Click the POS menu to the right of the search bar

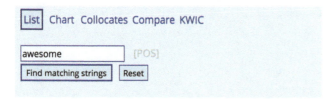

Step 3: Select prep.ALL from the drop-down menu

This will place what is called a POS tag after your search word. Be sure there is a space between the word and the tag.

Step 4: Click *Find matching strings*

		CONTEXT	FREQ
1	☐	AWESOME IN	32
2	☐	AWESOME FOR	32
3	☐	AWESOME AT	22
4	☐	AWESOME TO	11
5	☐	AWESOME ON	8

As we have said, the corpus does not simply deliver you the answer. However, if you click on the items in the list, you will be able to see different patterns and uses of *awesome + preposition* and you will notice that *awesome in* and *awesome at* are rather different meanings. After looking at concordance lines, you will be able to create your own sentence that reflects the meaning that you want.

YOUR TURN 1.7

Think of a noun that you often see or hear in academic settings. Do a *part-of-speech (POS) search* to see examples of the different *noun + preposition* patterns in which it appears.

Search 8: How *awesome* is it?

We know that *awesome* is an adjective and that adverbs are used to modify adjectives. It could be interesting to discover which adverbs are most often used with an adjective.

Step 1: Click *List*

Step 2: Click the POS menu and select adv.ALL

Step 3: Enter *awesome* after the adv.ALL POS tag

Step 4: Click *Find matching strings*

		CONTEXT	FREQ
1	☐	SO AWESOME	104
2	☐	PRETTY AWESOME	92
3	☐	JUST AWESOME	74
4	☐	MOST AWESOME	67
5	☐	HOW AWESOME	54
6	☐	REALLY AWESOME	53
7	☐	TOTALLY AWESOME	52
8	☐	TRULY AWESOME	26
9	☐	MORE AWESOME	25
10	☐	AS AWESOME	25

YOUR TURN 1.8

POS searches can also be used to help us search for a word for when it is used as a particular word class. For example, *cook* can be used as both a noun and a verb. Let's see how to do searches that would separate the noun and verb uses of the word.

1. Search for cook as a noun. To complete this search, enter cook in the search bar and add the noun.ALL tag from the POS drop-down menu. Your search should look like this: cook.[nn*]

   Tip: Add a period, or full stop, after cook. There should not be space in-between the search word and the tag for this search. Recall in search 7 that we put a space between the word and the tag; this gave us the results for the word plus the POS.

2. Search for cook as a verb. To complete this search, put cook inside brackets like this: [cook] and then add the verb POS tag. We add the [ ] around cook to tell the corpus to search for all forms of cook as a verb (for example, cook, cooks, cooked, cooking). Your search should look like this: [cook].[v*]

3. Think of another word that is used as different parts of speech. Perform searches similar to those above to compare the frequency of your word in its different forms.

4. Briefly explain your findings.

   _____

   _____

   _____

   _____

   _____

   We will see more applications for this type of POS search in later chapters.

Search 9: Do people say *awesomeness*?

You may also be interested to discover what other words begin with *awe* or other ways in which *awesome* is used. For instance, did I really hear someone say *awesomeness* at the coffee shop today? Can I say *awesomely*? The search function that will help us answer these questions is called a *wildcard* search. For example, if you enter *comp**, you will get a list of words which begin with *comp-* (for example, *computer, company, complete, compare*). In contrast, if you enter **ness*, you will get a list of words which end with *-ness.*

Step 1: Click *List*

Step 2: Enter *awe* with the wildcard *

List	Chart Collocates Compare KWIC

awe*	[POS]

Find matching strings	Reset

Step 3: Click *Find matching strings*

		CONTEXT	FREQ
1	☐	AWESOME	5561
2	☐	AWE	3624
3	☐	AWED	885
4	☐	AWESTRUCK	383
5	☐	AWE-INSPIRING	360
6	☐	AWESOMELY	79
7	☐	AWESOMENESS	56
8	☐	AWE-STRUCK	48
9	☐	AWEIGH	37
10	☐	AWENA	31

Step 4: Return to the main search page and enter *some

List Chart Collocates Compare KWIC

*some   [POS]
Find matching strings   Reset

Step 5: Click *Find matching strings*

		CONTEXT	FREQ
1	○	SOME	876499
2	○	HANDSOME	9802
3	○	AWESOME	5556
4	○	TROUBLESOME	1811
5	○	GRUESOME	1560
6	○	WORRISOME	1474
7	○	CUMBERSOME	1252
8	○	WHOLESOME	1214
9	○	CHROMOSOME	1106
10	○	LONESOME	1019

YOUR TURN 1.9

Think of a common word stem that forms part of many words. For example, we could state that *friend* is a stem of *friendship*, *friendly*, and *friendliness*. Do a wildcard search to find the different forms of two different words.

Tip: Remember to add the wildcard *****

Word stem 1: _____

Top 5 forms of the word:

1)_____ 2)_____ 3)_____ 4)_____ 5)_____

Word stem 2: _____

Top 5 forms of the word:

1)_____ 2)_____ 3)_____ 4)_____ 5)_____

Search 10: Do British speakers say *awesome*?

To this point, we have only performed searches with an American English corpus. However, on this same site, we can also look at different varieties of English from countries around the world. It can be quite interesting to compare British and American language patterns to see how the two are different and think about why those differences may exist. It seems Americans are known for using the exclamation *awesome!*, but do British speakers use *awesome* too?

Step 1: Click the arrow in the bar at the top of the screen to exit the COCA

new Corpus of Contemporary American English ⓘ 📄 ⬇ ⤢			
SEARCH	FREQUENCY	CONTEXT	CHANGE/COMPARE

Step 2: Click *Go to BYU Corpus Portal*

Step 3: Click *British National Corpus (BNC)* from the list

You should notice that the interface for the BNC is exactly the same as the COCA. Thus, all the searches we have completed in the COCA can be completed the same way in the BNC. In general, these same search functions will work in all online corpora you find as well as build-your-own corpus tools you download online.

Step 4: Click *List*

Step 5: Enter *awesome* in the search bar and click *Find matching strings*

		CONTEXT	FREQ
1	○	AWESOME	366

Interesting! In the COCA, we discovered that *awesome* was used approximately 5,500 times in American English, but the BNC only has 366! We'll compare these two words more carefully in search 12.

Search 11: If British English users do not use *awesome*, what do they say?

Step 1: Click *List*

Step 2: Enter *[=awesome]* in the search bar

Step 3: Click *Find matching strings*

		CONTEXT	FREQ
1	☐	GRAND [S]	5432
2	☐	REMARKABLE [S]	3447
3	☐	TREMENDOUS [S]	1952
4	☐	AMAZING [S]	1809
5	☐	SPLENDID [S]	1638
6	☐	OVERWHELMING [S]	1312
7	☐	AWESOME [S]	366
8	☐	BREATHTAKING [S]	326
9	☐	FEARSOME [S]	234
10	☐	ASTOUNDING [S]	140

Search 12: Can I use the frequency number to compare the BNC and the COCA?

In a previous search, we were excited to discover such a difference in the use of *awesome* between British and American language users. However, we must be somewhat cautious with these results, as the numbers represent frequency, the total number of times a word is used in a corpus. Because the two corpora we compared are quite different in size (the COCA has over 560 million words while the BNC has 100 million), it would be more beneficial to compare the per million rate. In other words, let's compare how many times the words are used per million words in the two corpora. This is an important step when drawing conclusions about how two words are used differently in corpora of different sizes.

Step 1: In the COCA, click *Chart* and enter *awesome* in the search bar

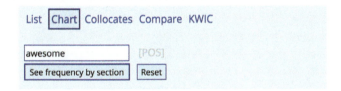

Step 2: Click *See frequency by section*

SECTION (CLICK FOR SUB-SECTIONS) (SEE ALL SECTIONS AT ONCE)	FREQ	SIZE (M)	PER MIL
SPOKEN	1850	109.4	16.91
FICTION	779	104.9	7.43
MAGAZINE	1496	110.1	13.59
NEWSPAPER	1090	106.0	10.29
ACADEMIC	341	103.4	3.30

Step 3: Go to the BNC and complete the same search

SECTION (CLICK FOR SUB-SECTIONS) (SEE ALL SECTIONS AT ONCE)	FREQ	SIZE (M)	PER MIL
SPOKEN	4	10.0	0.40
FICTION	84	15.9	5.28
MAGAZINE	58	7.3	7.99
NEWSPAPER	66	10.5	6.31
NON-ACAD	49	16.5	2.97
ACADEMIC	16	15.3	1.04
MISC	89	20.8	4.27

Now, using the charts produced in the COCA and the BNC, we can more accurately compare the use of *awesome*. We can still conclude that *awesome* is used much more frequently in American English and that the word is used most often in speaking.

YOUR TURN 1.10

Compare the use of modal verbs such as *can, could, may, ought to, might, should,* and *shall* in the COCA and the BNC. Before you begin your searches, answer the following questions.

1. Which modal do you think is most frequent in American English?

_____

2. Which modal do you think is least frequent in American English?

_____

3. Most frequent in British English?

_____

4. Least frequent in British English?

_____

5. Do you believe there will be a significant difference between the use of modals in American English and British English? Why?

_____

_____

_____

Find the per million rate for 5 modals and record the numbers in the chart.

Modal	PM in COCA	PM in BNC

Briefly summarise your findings and consider whether your original intuitions are supported by the corpus data.

_____

_____

_____

_____

_____

Search 13: Are Americans the only English speakers that use *awesome* so often?

Certainly, English is spoken in many more places than only the United States and the United Kingdom. The corpus collection we have been using also includes a massive corpus (approximately 2 billion words!) of internet texts from 20 countries. This corpus makes it possible for us to compare English language usage from English-speaking countries around the world.

Step 1: From the main search page, select the Global Web-based English Corpus (GloWbE)

corpus.byu.edu

corpora, size, queries = better resources, more insight

Created by Mark Davies, BYU. Overview, search types, looking at variation, corpus-based resources, updates.

The most widely used online corpora -- more than 130,000 distinct researchers, teachers, and students each month.

English	# words	language/dialect	time period	compare
NOW Corpus NEW	2.8 billion+	20 countries / Web	2010-yesterday	
Global Web-Based English (GloWbE)	1.9 billion	20 countries / Web	2012-13	
Wikipedia Corpus	1.9 billion	English	-2014	Info
Hansard Corpus (British Parliament)	1.6 billion	British	1803-2005	Info
Corpus of Contemporary American English (COCA)	520 million	American	1990-2015	★ ★ ★ ★ ★
Corpus of Historical American English (COHA)	400 million	American	1810-2009	★ ★
TIME Magazine Corpus	100 million	American	1923-2006	
Corpus of American Soap Operas	100 million	American	2001-2012	★
British National Corpus (BYU-BNC)*	100 million	British	1980s-1993	★ ★
Strathy Corpus (Canada)	50 million	Canadian	1970s-2000s	
CORE Corpus NEW	50 million	Web registers	-2014	
Other languages				
Corpus del Español (see also...)	100 million	Spanish	1200s-1900s	★
Corpus do Português (see also...)	45 million	Portuguese	1300s-1900s	
N-grams				
Google Books: American English	155 billion	American	1500s-2000s	★
Google Books: British English	34 billion	British	1500s-2000s	
Google Books: One Million Books	89 billion	Am/Br	1500s-2000s	
Google Books: Spanish	45 billion	Spanish	1500s-2000s	

Step 2: Click *Chart* and enter *awesome* in the search bar

Step 3: Click *See frequency by section*

SECTION	FREQ	SIZE (M)	PER MIL	CLICK FOR CONTEXT (SEE ALL)
United States	24987	386.8	64.60	
Canada	8872	134.8	65.83	
Great Britain	11787	387.6	30.41	
Ireland	2265	101.0	22.42	
Australia	8842	148.2	59.66	
New Zealand	5208	81.4	63.99	
India	3393	96.4	35.19	
Sri Lanka	873	46.6	18.74	
Pakistan	1338	51.4	26.05	
Bangladesh	1074	39.5	27.20	
Singapore	3829	43.0	89.10	
Malaysia	2489	41.6	59.77	
Philippines	2409	43.2	55.70	
Hong Kong	1392	40.5	34.41	
South Africa	2858	45.4	63.00	
Nigeria	867	42.6	20.33	
Ghana	685	38.8	17.67	
Kenya	1256	41.1	30.59	
Tanzania	900	35.2	25.60	
Jamaica	1244	39.6	31.44	

The search of the GloWbE again shows the value of looking at per million rate when making comparisons. We can see though that several countries use *awesome* at a similar rate as the United States. Interestingly, Singapore uses it at the highest frequency. If we click on the blue bar next to Singapore, we can see examples of *awesome* from Singaporean web texts. This is an interesting result, and one that may not match our intuition. Showing us that our intuition about language is often not true and accurate is one of the great benefits of using corpora. While more textbooks are using corpus data to help create authentic samples for dialogues, and so on, you now have the power to test your own intuition and answer your own questions. The next time you are waiting to ask your teacher about a word or phrase, try asking the corpus instead.

YOUR TURN 1.11

Test your intuition about a word you have heard or read recently. Write a word in the blank below. Answer the question according to your intuition. Then, do corpus searches and test whether your intuition is accurate.

Word: _____

1. In what register (for example, spoken, fiction, magazine, newspaper, academic) is the word used most frequently?

   Intuition:

   _____

   Corpus findings:

   _____

2. What do you think are the top 5 collocates that occur with the word?
   (Choose your collocation window carefully to narrow your results as you wish.)

   Intuition:

   _____

   Corpus findings:

   _____

3. Is the word used more frequently in the US or UK? *(Compare per million rate.)*

   Intuition:

   _____

   Corpus findings:

   _____

4. Briefly summarise the results and explain whether your intuition was accurate.

   _____

   _____

   _____

Before we continue, let's remember that corpora are compiled of different types of texts, often collected at different periods of time, and are typically different sizes. Before doing a corpus search, think carefully about which corpus is best to answer your language question for your context. For example, if you were revising an academic essay, you would not want to make a language choice based on your findings from a corpus of blogs.

Search 14: When did people start saying *awesome* often in the US?

Many people enjoy completing corpus searches that show when a particular word began to be used or how the use of a word has changed over time. These can be quite interesting as they can reveal much about how language changes and develops.

Step 1: Go to the corpus homepage and select the Corpus of Historical American English (COHA)

corpus.byu.edu

corpora, size, queries = better resources, more insight

Created by Mark Davies, BYU. Overview, search types, looking at variation, corpus-based resources, updates.

The most widely used online corpora -- more than 130,000 distinct researchers, teachers, and students each month.

English	# words	language/dialect	time period	compare
NOW Corpus NEW	2.8 billion+	20 countries / Web	2010-yesterday	
Global Web-Based English (GloWbE)	1.9 billion	20 countries / Web	2012-13	
Wikipedia Corpus	1.9 billion	English	-2014	Info
Hansard Corpus (British Parliament)	1.6 billion	British	1803-2005	Info
Corpus of Contemporary American English (COCA)	520 million	American	1990-2015	★★★★★
Corpus of Historical American English (COHA)	400 million	American	1810-2009	★★
TIME Magazine Corpus	100 million	American	1923-2006	
Corpus of American Soap Operas	100 million	American	2001-2012	★
British National Corpus (BYU-BNC)*	100 million	British	1980s-1993	★★
Strathy Corpus (Canada)	50 million	Canadian	1970s-2000s	
CORE Corpus NEW	50 million	Web registers	-2014	
Other languages				
Corpus del Español (see also...)	100 million	Spanish	1200s-1900s	★
Corpus do Português (see also...)	45 million	Portuguese	1300s-1900s	
N-grams				
Google Books: American English	155 billion	American	1500s-2000s	★
Google Books: British English	34 billion	British	1500s-2000s	
Google Books: One Million Books	89 billion	Am/Br	1500s-2000s	
Google Books: Spanish	45 billion	Spanish	1500s-2000s	

Step 2: Click *Chart* and enter *awesome* in the search bar

Step 3: Click *See frequency by section*

SECTION (CLICK FOR SUB-SECTIONS) (SEE ALL SECTIONS AT ONCE)	FREQ	SIZE (M)	PER MIL	CLICK FOR CONTEXT (SEE ALL)
1810	0	1.2	0.00	
1820	0	6.9	0.00	
1830	0	13.8	0.00	
1840	0	16.0	0.00	
1850	0	16.5	0.00	
1860	2	17.1	0.12	▮
1870	4	18.6	0.22	▪
1880	8	20.3	0.39	▬
1890	13	20.6	0.63	▬
1900	15	22.1	0.68	▬
1910	24	22.7	1.06	▬▬
1920	31	25.7	1.21	▬▬
1930	31	24.6	1.26	▬▬
1940	60	24.3	2.46	▬▬▬▬
1950	74	24.5	3.01	▬▬▬▬▬
1960	131	24.0	5.46	▬▬▬▬▬▬▬▬
1970	208	23.8	8.73	▬▬▬▬▬▬▬▬▬▬▬▬▬
1980	233	25.3	9.20	▬▬▬▬▬▬▬▬▬▬▬▬▬▬
1990	183	27.9	6.55	▬▬▬▬▬▬▬▬▬▬
2000	258	29.6	8.73	▬▬▬▬▬▬▬▬▬▬▬▬▬

In the chart, we can see that the first recorded uses of *awesome* were in the 1860s, the word was used increasingly more frequently for the next 100 years, and it reached its highest use in the 1980s. It looks like the 1990s were not so *awesome*, but the 2000s were better.

YOUR TURN 1.12

Think of another word whose popularity you feel has likely risen or fallen recently. Do a corpus search and explain the trend.

Word: _____

Findings:

_____

_____

_____

Searches of words and their changes over time can give insights into national, technological, cultural, and social changes. We will complete more of these searches using the COHA, the News on the Web (NOW) Corpus, and the Google Ngram Viewer in Chapter 4 on using corpus searches for cultural study.

These searches in Chapter 1 have shown us much about the word *awesome*. We learned the nouns it most commonly modifies, the adverbs which most often are used with it, how its usage differs between the US and the UK, and much more. Hopefully, through the additional 'Your Turn' searches you have also learned much more about many other words too. In the coming chapters, we will learn to apply these basic search principles to help us in a variety of situations. While we have learned much about corpora and corpus searches in Chapter 1, there are still many topics we have yet to discover. Much more to explore!

2 CORPUS SEARCHES FOR VOCABULARY LEARNING

IT IS LIKELY that the most common use of corpora amongst language learners is for vocabulary learning, and corpus use can certainly be a great way to complement your preparation for exams such as the GRE and TOEFL. While many students may first refer to a learner's dictionary or an app on their smart phone to quickly look up or translate a word, students can also use corpora to see sample sentences of a word, find synonyms, explore a word's use in different registers, or make word lists for their specific area of interest. One reason corpus study is beneficial is because it allows you to see multiple examples of a word being used in a variety of authentic contexts. Research shows that language learners need to encounter a word many times before they are able to produce it in their own speaking and writing, and corpus study can assist in this process. For example, imagine you hear the word *confiscate* while watching a crime drama on television. You can certainly look up the word in a dictionary to find its definition, but it can be more useful to expose yourself to many examples of the word in actual language use. Yes, you could read some crime novels and watch many more dramas to hear the word used again, or you can do a corpus search and find many examples from television news, sitcoms, newspapers, and more. In addition, by using the corpus, you don't need to wait and wait to ask your language teacher how or in what situations you can use a word. Instead of waiting, make 'To the corpus!' your mantra.

In this chapter, we'll explore several corpora and how each can be used for vocabulary learning. We will be following some of the same search techniques we used in the first chapter; however, the searches and activities in this section are focused specifically on vocabulary learning and how we can use corpus searches to create useful word lists to help us in our learning process.

Search 1: Learning words with shared roots

Many language learners often must take standardised tests such as the TOEFL or GRE, and your success in these exams will be greatly influenced by your vocabulary knowledge and fluency. While many strategies exist for vocabulary study, learners often try to divide vocabulary into meaningful groups. One way you can do this is by creating lists of words which share the same word root. For example, the root -*audi*- is in many words meaning to hear, the root -*jur*- is in words dealing with law and justice, and -*terr*- is in words referring to soil and earth. These are just a few of the many word roots that serve as the building blocks of the lexicon. By learning the roots and the words which include the root, you can efficiently learn a large number of words and also be able to better guess the meaning of newly encountered words. Let's find words which have the root -*audi*-.

Step 1: Go to the COCA and click the search function *List*

Step 2: Enter *audi** in the search box

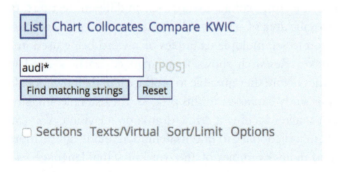

Tip: In Chapter 1, we discussed how to perform wildcard searches. Entering * in the search means we will get a list of a words that begin with the root in which we are interested but may have different endings.

Step 3: Review the list of words and make a list of the top 10 words which
include the root

		CONTEXT	FREQ	
1	☐	AUDIENCE	38966	
2	☐	AUDIENCES	8700	
3	☐	AUDIO	8452	
4	☐	AUDIT	4823	
5	☐	AUDITORIUM	3110	
6	☐	AUDITORY	2603	
7	☐	AUDITION	1962	
8	☐	AUDITORS	1907	
9	☐	AUDIBLE	1814	
10	☐	AUDITOR	1527	
11	☐	AUDIOTAPE	1427	
12	☐	AUDITS	1408	
13	☐	AUDITING	1130	
14	☐	AUDI	915	
15	☐	AUDITIONS	750	

Step 4: Click on an unfamiliar word in the list to view example sentences

cuts that would neither bleed nor heal and could only be glued. And the audible creaking of his joints, and the dryness of his eyes and mouth he had

bank. Without quite saying it, and even after lowering his voice to an audible whisper, it was clear that this important person was the head of a crime

the heel of his hands. The same flat thud came from it, barely audible in the thundering around him. " Heart and soul, brother, " the

is what a driver should feel like when you catch the sweet spot; the audible click at impact is what you expect from Titleist; misses aren't painful,

and carrying a large underwater video camera with hydrophones. He records several seconds of audible chirping between Hector and Han, then his cam

YOUR TURN 2.1

Think of another word root and do a wildcard search using * to find words which share the root. If you cannot think of a word root, do a quick internet search for 'common word roots' or use one of the roots included in the discussion.

Root: _____

1. What is the meaning of the root?

2. List 6–8 words that share the same root:

1._____2. _____3. _____

4. _____ 5. _____6. _____

7. _____ 8. _____

3. For the list of words sharing the root -audi-, it is possible to apply the category 'words referring to sounds and hearing'. Create a label for the word group generated through your search:

_____

Search 2: Learning words with the same endings

In search 1, we looked for roots that are used at the beginning of words. It can also be useful to create lists of words which share common endings.

Step 1: Enter *ize in the search bar

Because the COCA is a corpus of American English, use the -ize spelling rather than the British -ise form.

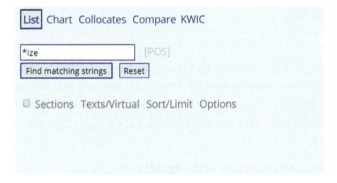

Step 2: Click the POS menu that appears next to the search bar

Step 3: When the menu appears, click verb.ALL

The POS tag will appear in the search bar.

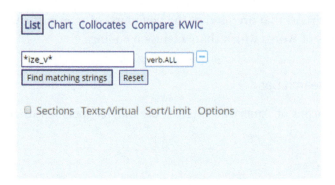

An important part of doing corpus searches is learning how to narrow your searches to produce more focused and beneficial results. If you are not able to create focused searches, the information may not help you to answer the question you have. Think for a moment: what will our results be for the search *ize_v*?

Step 4: Click *Find matching strings* and view the results

You will notice that we get a list of only verbs that end with *ize rather than a list of all words that end with *ize. Applying POS tags is one method to focus our results, and creating a list of only verbs that end in *ize can be useful. As you continue your searches, explore the POS tags and how adding them to your searches can help you find the information for which you are searching.

		CONTEXT	FREQ	
1		REALIZE	33571	
2		RECOGNIZE	28547	
3		EMPHASIZE	8101	
4		ORGANIZE	7290	
5		MINIMIZE	5924	
6		APOLOGIZE	5679	
7		CRITICIZE	3807	
8		MAXIMIZE	3648	
9		SEIZE	3435	
10		CHARACTERIZE	3327	
11		UTILIZE	2686	
12		STABILIZE	2600	
13		MOBILIZE	1863	
14		CAPITALIZE	1673	
15		SPECIALIZE	1569	

YOUR TURN 2.2

Think of another ending that is shared by many words. If you cannot think of another example, do a search with the word ending *-tion*, *-ism*, or *-tive*. Remember to use the wildcard for your search. Create a list of the top 10 most frequent words which use the word ending.

Word ending: _____

High-frequency words:

1._____2. _____3. _____

4. _____ 5. _____6. _____

7. _____ 8. _____9. _____

10. _____

Do the words in the list have anything in common? For example, are they all the same part of speech? Explain.

_____

_____

_____

_____

Search 3: Learning descriptive adjectives

In this search, you can learn how to identify the adjectives which are commonly used with a particular noun. Since many of you are likely learning English for academic purposes, let's do a search for a frequent academic word and the adjectives which are often used to modify it.

Step 1: Click the POS menu next to the search bar and click on the adj.
        ALL tag

This step will add j* to the search bar to help us focus our search results. We could simply use the wildcard * in this position, but this would cause many non-adjectives to appear in our list. Again, let's think carefully about the search so that our results are focused.

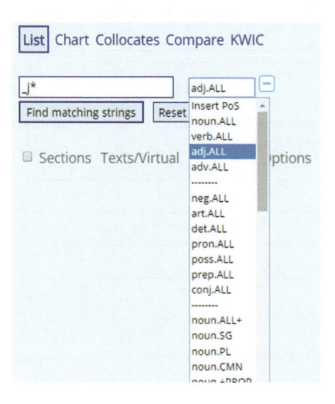

Step 2: Enter *study* in the search box

There should be a space in-between '_j*' and *study*. The syntax of these searches is very important to produce accurate results.

Step 3: Click the POS menu again and select noun.ALL

This will again help us to narrow our results. If we do not add the noun.ALL tag following study, our list will include items where study may be used as other forms. In this case, there is NOT a space between study and the POS tag nn*. This is important to remember: if there is a space between the word and the POS tag, the corpus will produce results that display two words (for example, an adjective plus the word *study*). If there is no space between the word and the POS tag, the corpus searches for examples of the word as the POS which you selected. Thus, the search below will produce a list of frequent adjective + study (when used as noun) pairs.

List Chart Collocates Compare KWIC

_j* study_nn*   noun.ALL ⊟

Find matching strings   Reset

☐ Sections Texts/Virtual Sort/Limit Options

Step 4: Click *Find matching strings*

Step 5: View results

The results display the adjectives *present, current, recent, new,* and *longitudinal*. It seems clear from the list that academic writers believe it is important to indicate the timeliness of a study. Further review of the list reveals other qualities that academic writers view as important characteristics of a study such as *longitudinal, qualitative, exploratory,* and *independent*. Perhaps you are asking, 'What is a longitudinal study?' Click on the phrase to read sample sentences and determine the meaning.

		CONTEXT	FREQ	
1	☐	PRESENT STUDY	6696	████████████████
2	☐	CURRENT STUDY	3234	████████
3	☐	RECENT STUDY	2619	██████
4	☐	NEW STUDY	1693	████
5	☐	LONGITUDINAL STUDY	901	██
6	☐	FURTHER STUDY	723	██
7	☐	PREVIOUS STUDY	425	■
8	☐	SCIENTIFIC STUDY	407	■
9	☐	QUALITATIVE STUDY	320	■
10	☐	NATIONAL STUDY	314	■
11	☐	FOLLOW-UP STUDY	290	■
12	☐	LARGER STUDY	286	■
13	☐	EXPLORATORY STUDY	284	■
14	☐	INDEPENDENT STUDY	268	■
15	☐	EARLIER STUDY	267	■

YOUR TURN 2.3

You completed a search that displayed the common adjectives that are used in the academic register to modify and describe *study*. Think of another noun that is important for a particular context and do a similar search to the one we have just completed. For example, you could search for *research* as a noun to discover how people at universities discuss their own and others' research. Or you could choose a frequent noun used in business such as *investor* or *report* and investigate the common adjectives which are used to describe it.

Noun: _____

High-frequency adjectives:

1._____2. _____3. _____

4. _____ 5. _____6. _____

Search 4: More with adjectives

While the previous search helped us learn the common descriptive adjectives used with a particular noun, this search will enable us to make a list of adjectives that have a common ending. For this search, let's create a list of adjectives that end in -*ive*.

Step 1: Enter *ive

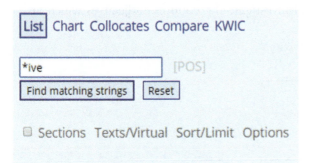

Step 2: Click the POS menu and select adj.ALL

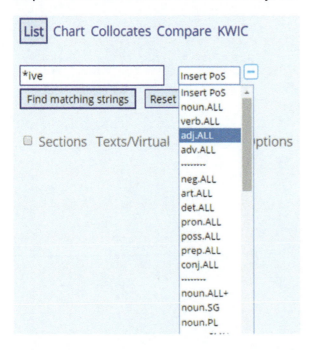

We are adding the adj.ALL tag so that our results will be only adjectives that end in *ive*.

If we don't add the POS tag, our list will include many words such as *give* and *drive* that are not adjectives.

Step 3: Click *Find matching strings*

Step 4: View results

		CONTEXT	FREQ	
1		POSITIVE	54325	
2		EFFECTIVE	48767	
3		NATIVE	35962	
4		ACTIVE	35228	
5		NEGATIVE	35221	
6		ALIVE	31958	
7		EXPENSIVE	28325	
8		CONSERVATIVE	27049	
9		LIVE	24593	
10		MASSIVE	24133	
11		CREATIVE	23119	
12		COMPETITIVE	18596	
13		ALTERNATIVE	17039	
14		AGGRESSIVE	16918	
15		SENSITIVE	16863	

Once you see the results, it can be useful to make lists of the top 5, top 10, or top 20 words on the list. As you study the list, click on unknown words to get example sentences. If you are studying vocabulary for academic purposes, complete the same search but use the *Chart* search function (see the image below). By using this search option, you can find examples of these words used in sentences in academic writing. Click on the blue bars under *Click for context* to see authentic examples of these words in use in that particular register.

SECTION (CLICK FOR SUB-SECTIONS) (SEE ALL SECTIONS AT ONCE)	FREQ	SIZE (M)	PER MIL	CLICK FOR CONTEXT (SEE ALL)
SPOKEN	139,082	109.4	1,271.41	
FICTION	79,498	104.9	757.84	
MAGAZINE	232,024	110.1	2,107.19	
NEWSPAPER	202,968	106.0	1,915.45	
ACADEMIC	452,360	103.4	4,373.93	

YOUR TURN 2.4

You have completed a search to help you discover and learn adjectives ending in *ive and then narrowed your results to find sample sentences from the academic register. Do a similar search using the common adverb ending -ly. What are the top 5 adverbs ending in -ly in the academic register?

Tip: If you ever experience search errors while using the corpus, click the Reset button.

Top 5 adverbs:

1. _____

2. _____

3. _____

4. _____

5. _____

Search 5: Finding lemmas

This search is rather easy, but it is an important one to know how to do. Before the search, we need to understand what a **lemma** is. A lemma is the base form of a word of which there are many variations. For example, *takes*, *took*, and *taking* are related to the lemma *take*. Let's illustrate that idea with a quick search.

Step 1: Click *List*

Step 2: Enter *[take]* in the search bar

List	Chart Collocates Compare KWIC

[take]   [POS]

Find matching strings   Reset

☐ Sections Texts/Virtual Sort/Limit Options

Step 3: Click *Find matching strings*

| | SEARCH | | FREQUENCY | | CONTEXT | | HELP | |

SEE CONTEXT: CLICK ON WORD OR SELECT WORDS + [CONTEXT] [HELP...]   COMPARE

	■	CONTEXT	FREQ	
1	☐	TAKE	383038	
2	☐	TOOK	201179	
3	☐	TAKING	111302	
4	☐	TAKEN	107291	
5	☐	TAKES	82766	
6	☐	TAKIN	301	
		TOTAL	885877	

Your results will show you a list of all of the forms of the main verb *take*. For instance, we will see frequencies for *take*, *took*, *taking*, *taken*, *takes*, and even the slang form *takin*. This is a useful search function because we may want to discover what words are often used with all forms of *take* or quickly compare two forms such as the participle *taken* and the simple past *took*. It would require too much time if we had to do those searches individually for all the different forms.

Step 4: With *[take]* still in the search bar, click *Collocates* and set the collocation window at 0L–4R

Here is an example of how adjusting the collocation window can be useful. We may not be interested in who *takes, took,* or *has taken* (for example, he, she, Geoffrey) but rather what sorts of things people *take, took,* or *are taking* (for example, naps, breaks, time). Thus, adjusting the window helps us get exactly the results we want.

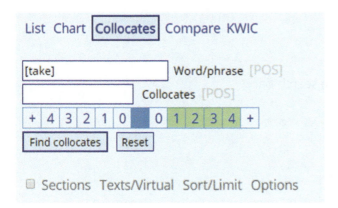

Step 5: Click *Find collocates*

		CONTEXT	FREQ	ALL	%	MI	
1		PLACE	32880	251124	13.09	4.30	
2		OFF	30268	382410	7.92	3.58	
3		CARE	26532	166639	15.92	4.58	
4		LOOK	18028	334458	5.39	3.02	
5		AWAY	16105	259256	6.21	3.23	
6		ADVANTAGE	11667	30104	38.76	5.87	
7		SERIOUSLY	8744	24053	36.35	5.78	
8		BREAK	8505	81505	10.43	3.97	
9		STEP	7696	67539	11.39	4.10	
10		STEPS	6767	44753	15.12	4.51	
11		ACTION	6674	75427	8.85	3.74	
12		BREATH	6533	31627	20.66	4.96	
13		ACCOUNT	6214	42133	14.75	4.47	
14		DEEP	5449	67952	8.02	3.59	
15		RESPONSIBILITY	4362	36709	11.88	4.16	

Scan the collocates list and click on items that you are not certain of how they are used or what they mean. For example, *[take]* + *place* is the most common collocation. If you do not know what this means, click on *place* to see example sentences and try to determine what the phrase means.

YOUR TURN 2.5

Lemma searches are useful for vocabulary learning but can help with understanding grammar too. If you are having difficulty deciding when to use a present perfect verb (*have lived*), the past perfect (*had lived*), and the simple past (*lived*), you can do a lemma search to quickly see examples for each. This can help you determine how these three forms are different and when each is appropriate. Complete a lemma search for an irregular verb such as *forget*. Scan the concordance lines for several of its forms.

Search 6: Searching for synonyms and comparing their
                usage in different registers

One of the many great features of corpus study is the ability to compare the use
of a word in different registers. For example, you may want to see how the use of
a **linking adverbial** such as *however*, *moreover*, or *therefore* differs between spoken
and academic registers. For this search, let's investigate how the use of a particular adjective and its synonyms differs between academic and business registers.

Step 1: Enter *=new* in the search bar

Entering an equals sign next to a search word produces a list of synonyms.

Step 2: Click *Sections*

List Chart Collocates Compare KWIC

=new   [POS]

Find matching strings   Reset

☐ Sections Sort/Limit Options

Step 3: When the drop-down menu appears, click *Academic* in the first
         column and *Fiction* in the second column

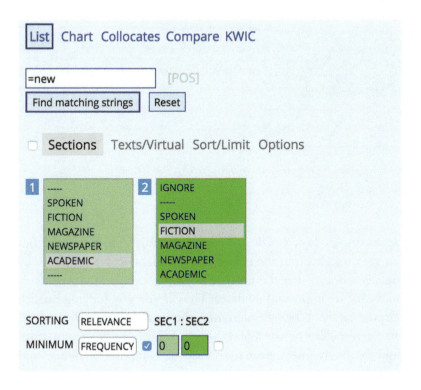

Step 4: Click *Find matching strings*

Step 5: View and compare results for synonyms of *new* in the two registers

SEE CONTEXT: CLICK ON WORD (ALL SECTIONS) OR NUMBER (SPECIFIED SECTION)   [HELP...]

SEC 1 (ACADEMIC): 103,421,981 WORDS

	WORD/PHRASE	TOKENS 1	TOKENS 2	PM 1	PM 2	RATIO
1	INNOVATIVE	3326	141	32.2	1.3	23.9
2	ADDITIONAL	18777	1074	181.6	10.2	17.7
3	CONTEMPORARY	13130	754	127.0	7.2	17.7
4	RECENT	26392	3822	255.2	36.4	7.0
5	MODERN	18605	3061	179.9	29.2	6.2
6	FURTHER	35202	7520	340.4	71.7	4.7
7	UP-TO-DATE	467	105	4.5	1.0	4.5
8	ORIGINAL	14462	4261	139.8	40.6	3.4
9	DIFFERENT	68185	23972	659.3	228.5	2.9
10	NOVEL	11271	3972	109.0	37.9	2.9
11	INEXPERIENCED	462	228	4.5	2.2	2.1
12	NEW	151705	76559	1,466.9	729.8	2.0
13	FIRSTHAND	514	269	5.0	2.6	1.9
14	MORE	267236	165631	2,583.9	1,578.9	1.6
15	OTHER	202476	129069	1,957.8	1,230.4	1.6

SEC 2 (FICTION): 104,900,827 WORDS

	WORD/PHRASE	TOKENS 2	TOKENS 1	PM 2	PM 1	RATIO
1	BRAND-NEW	600	70	5.7	0.7	8.5
2	GREEN	22720	7048	216.6	68.1	3.2
3	UNACCUSTOMED	299	95	2.9	0.9	3.1
4	NEWFANGLED	46	15	0.4	0.1	3.0
5	FRESH	8641	2897	82.4	28.0	2.9
6	SPANKING	127	49	1.2	0.5	2.6
7	EXTRA	5455	3246	52.0	31.4	1.7
8	PRISTINE	545	341	5.2	3.3	1.6
9	NEWBORN	718	460	6.8	4.4	1.5
10	ANOTHER	77575	54837	739.5	530.2	1.4
11	LATEST	3170	2534	30.2	24.5	1.2
12	NEWFOUND	270	267	2.6	2.6	1.0
13	UNFAMILIAR	1458	1557	13.9	15.1	0.9
14	UP-TO-THE-MINUTE	19	22	0.2	0.2	0.9
15	MODERNISTIC	12	16	0.1	0.2	0.7

These results again display how words are used differently across contexts but also how we can gain insights into the values and practices of a community by studying its language choices. For the academic list, we can see that *innovative*, *contemporary*, and *modern* are important qualities. Thus, if you are studying English for academic purposes, it seems beneficial to study the vocabulary which academics use rather than general lists of vocabulary words. While we did a comparison of academic and fiction registers, you may wish to compare academic and spoken registers instead.

YOUR TURN 2.6

In the opening pages of this book, you discovered that although *beautiful* and *attractive* appear to be synonyms they are used quite differently. In this search, you were able to focus on how an adjective is used to modify different types of nouns. Think of another common adjective and investigate how it is used differently between the academic and spoken register.

Adjective: _____

How is the adjective used differently in the two registers? In other words, what are the differences in the words with which it is used?

_____

_____

_____

_____

Search 7: Close reading with wordandphrase.info

The first searches in this chapter used a large general corpus of American English, although some of our searches did use sub-corpora of certain registers. However, for the next few searches, we'll be using wordandphrase.info. This site is more focused for academic purposes and will be a great tool for those learning English to continue your studies at an English medium university. One of the most useful functions of this site is that it allows you to enter your own texts for study. You likely read many online texts in English as part of your studies. What do you do when you encounter a word that you don't know? Maybe you look up the word quickly in a dictionary or perhaps you try to guess the meaning of the word based on the context. These are both good strategies, but wordandphrase. info can do much more and it can do so more quickly.

Step 1: Open a new window and go to https://www.wordandphrase.info

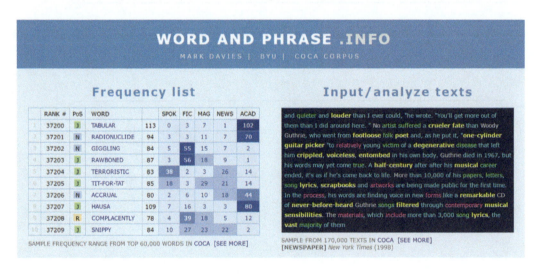

Step 2: Click the option on the right side of the screen that says *Input/ Analyze texts*

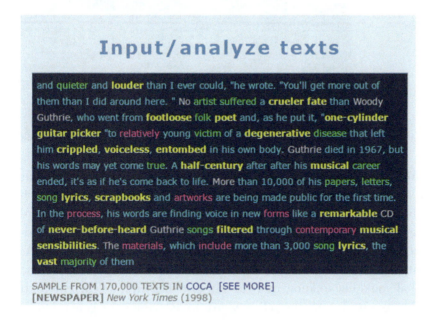

Input/analyze texts

and quieter and **louder** than I ever could, "he wrote. "You'll get more out of them than I did around here. " No artist suffered a **crueler fate** than Woody Guthrie, who went from **footloose** folk **poet** and, as he put it, **"one-cylinder guitar picker** "to relatively young victim of a **degenerative** disease that left him **crippled, voiceless, entombed** in his own body. Guthrie died in 1967, but his words may yet come true. A **half-century** after after his **musical** career ended, it's as if he's come back to life. More than 10,000 of his papers, letters, song **lyrics, scrapbooks** and artworks are being made public for the first time. In the process, his words are finding voice in new forms like a **remarkable** CD of **never-before-heard** Guthrie songs **filtered** through contemporary **musical sensibilities**. The materials, which include more than 3,000 song **lyrics**, the **vast** majority of them

SAMPLE FROM 170,000 TEXTS IN COCA [SEE MORE]
[NEWSPAPER] *New York Times* (1998)

Step 3: Click on the *Samples* menu and select *Acad* for academic

The sample text changes each time it is selected. Thus, you will see a different text in your searches. This search highlights how you can use the site, but to fully benefit from the site you should copy and paste texts which you are reading into the text box.

ENTER TEXT BELOW   -SAMPLES- ▼   MY TEXTS

-SAMPLES-
FIC
MAG
NEWS
ACAD

LEARNER 1
LEARNER 2
LEARNER 3
LEARNER 4
LEARNER 5

SEARCH   CLEAR   H   ● WORD   ○ PHRASE

Step 4: Click *Search*

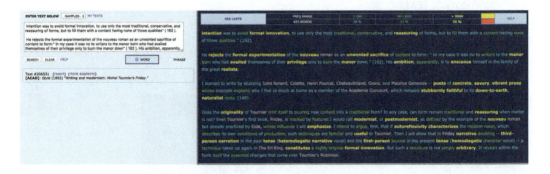

In the window on the right side of the screen, you will be able to view the texts with many of the words highlighted. The words in aqua are words which commonly appear in English texts, the words in green are less common, and the words in yellow are more specialised. The words in yellow can be considered more academic and will mostly occur in academic writing and lectures. As you encounter an unknown word whose meaning you can't guess from the context or that you'd like to know more about, just click on it to learn more. It is also possible to quickly scan the yellow words to determine the general topic of the text.

Step 5: Click on a green or yellow word from the first line of the article

In this example, the word *innovation* was selected.

Step 6: View results in the bottom section of the screen

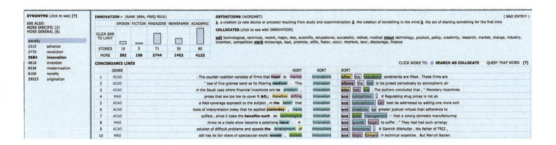

Once you click on a word, you are provided with a lot of helpful information. You can view synonyms of the word, a chart displaying its use in different registers, the definition, its common collocates, and concordance lines with different parts of speech colour coded. In the above results, we can quickly determine that *an advance* is a common synonym of *innovation,* that *innovation* is most frequently used in academic writing, and that *technological* is its most common adjective collocate. And all of this in one place as you read your article!

YOUR TURN 2.7

Add a text to wordandphrase.info which you have read recently or perhaps one that you were asked to read in class. You could even copy one of your own essays in the search box.

Once you have added your text, click *Search* and view the results. Choose a word from your text that maybe you have noticed but that you don't know well. Complete the following.

Word: _____

Definition: _____

common synonyms:

_____, _____, _____, _____

collocates:

_____, _____, _____, _____

In which register is the word most frequently used? _____

Search 8: More with wordandphrase.info

The other main function wordandphrase.info allows is word searches similar to those we have completed in the COCA. However, while the COCA makes possible many different search types for many different purposes, wordandphrase. info is designed primarily for language study. For that reason, you may feel that the interface is more user-friendly and the results easier to sort. Both sites have different strengths, but for some searches you may like using wordandphrase.info more than the COCA.

Step 1: Click *Frequency list* at the top left of the wordandphrase.info homepage

Frequency list

	RANK #	PoS	WORD		SPOK	FIC	MAG	NEWS	ACAD
1	37200	J	TABULAR	113	0	3	7	1	102
2	37201	N	RADIONUCLIDE	94	3	3	11	7	70
3	37202	N	GIGGLING	84	5	55	15	7	2
4	37203	J	RAWBONED	87	3	56	18	9	1
5	37204	J	TERRORISTIC	83	38	2	3	26	14
6	37205	J	TIT-FOR-TAT	85	18	3	29	21	14
7	37206	N	ACCRUAL	80	2	6	10	18	44
8	37207	J	HAUSA	109	7	16	3	3	80
9	37208	R	COMPLACENTLY	78	4	39	18	5	12
10	37209	J	SNIPPY	84	10	27	23	22	2

SAMPLE FREQUENCY RANGE FROM TOP 60,000 WORDS IN COCA [SEE MORE]

Step 2: Enter *defer* in the search box

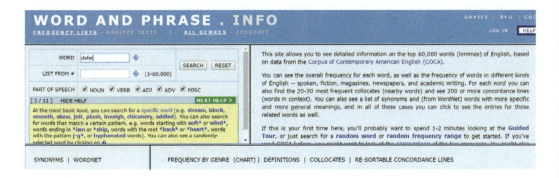

Step 3: Click the *Search* button

Step 4: View results

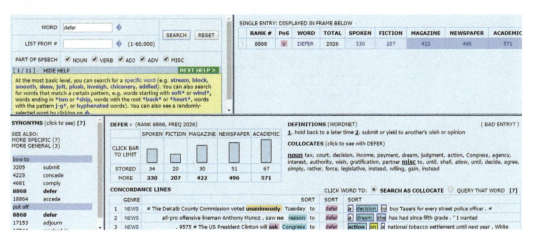

As with the previous search on wordandphrase.info, you are presented with a lot of information about your search word. Notice at the top of the page you can view the frequency of the word in various registers and that *defer* is most common in academic writing. You can also see the types of things people often defer: *taxes, decisions,* and *income.*

Step 5: Click on the number under *Academic* in the chart

SINGLE ENTRY: DISPLAYED IN FRAME BELOW

	RANK #	PoS	WORD	TOTAL	SPOKEN	FICTION	MAGAZINE	NEWSPAPER	ACADEMIC
1	8868	V	DEFER	2026	330	207	422	496	<u>571</u>

Because you clicked on this number, you will notice that all of the concordance lines are now from academic writing. In addition to the definition, collocates, and synonyms, you can also view samples of your word in the specific context in which you are interested.

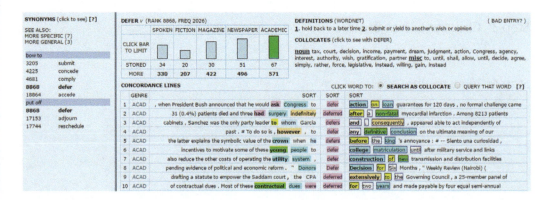

YOUR TURN 2.8

Choose another word and explore! Explain your findings.

Word: _____

Findings:

_____

_____

_____

_____

Search 9: Creating specialised word lists

The COCA and wordandphrase.info are great resources that are ready for you to use. However, you may feel that a word list focused more specifically on your area of study would be more useful. Maybe you would rather study only the most frequent words in biology, engineering, or economics. Fortunately, that's also possible!

Step 1: Return to https://corpus.byu.edu and enter the Wikipedia Corpus

English	# words	language/dialect	time period	compare
NOW Corpus	2.8 billion+	20 countries / Web	2010-yesterday	
Global Web-Based English (GloWbE)	1.9 billion	20 countries / Web	2012-13	
Wikipedia Corpus	1.9 billion	English	-2014	Info
Hansard Corpus (British Parliament)	1.6 billion	British	1803-2005	Info
Corpus of Contemporary American English (COCA)	520 million	American	1990-2015	★ ★ ★ ★ ★
Corpus of Historical American English (COHA)	400 million	American	1810-2009	★ ★
Corpus of US Supreme Court Opinions NEW	130 million	American	1790s-present	
TIME Magazine Corpus	100 million	American	1923-2006	
Corpus of American Soap Operas	100 million	American	2001-2012	★
British National Corpus (BYU-BNC)*	100 million	British	1980s-1993	★ ★
Strathy Corpus (Canada)	50 million	Canadian	1970s-2000s	
CORE Corpus	50 million	Web registers	-2014	

Step 2: Click *Texts/Virtual* and select *Create corpus*

List   Collocates Compare KWIC

[   ] [POS]
Find matching strings   Reset

Texts/Virtual   Sort/Limit Options

SEARCH ALL   Create corpus
FIND ARTICLES
MY CORPORA   Edit corpora
....
                 Find keywords

                 Refresh list

Step 3: Enter *economics* in the search bar next to *Title word(s)*

Title word(s) *	economics
	(See examples)
(Optional) Words **not** in title	
	(See examples)
(Optional) Words in pages	
	(See examples)
(Optional) Words **not** in pages	
	(See examples)
# pages	100

Submit   Reset

This search will compile a corpus of all pages on Wikipedia that include the word *economics*. You can choose your field of study (for example, engineering or philosophy) or an area of interest (for example, jazz or cycling).

Step 4: Click *Submit*

You will now see a page listing 100 Wikipedia pages which include *economics* in the title.

SAVE AS: economics	OR ADD TO: --SELECT--	SUBMIT	RESET		
HELP	☐ 100	# WORDS ↕	↕	↕	TITLE (SEE IN WIKIPEDIA) ↕
1	☑	11,019	6782	313	Economics
2	☑	6,053	2893	195	London School of Economics
3	☑	1,809	635	68	Capital (economics)
4	☑	2,856	542	110	Service (economics)
5	☑	1,845	522	46	Market (economics)
6	☑	1,624	361	28	Profit (economics)
7	☑	1,359	333	35	Home economics
8	☑	1,231	332	27	Good (economics)
9	☑	950	289	105	Philosophy, Politics and Economics
10	☑	4,293	278	96	Keynesian economics

Step 5: Enter *economics* in the box next to *Save as* and click *Submit*

You now have created your own specialised corpus on the topic of economics for you to use in your studies. This can be tremendously useful!

MY VIRTUAL CORPORA

HELP		↕	↕	LIST NAME ↕	# ARTICLES ↕	# WORDS ↕	FIND KEYWORDS ◉ SPECIFIC ○ FREQ	CREATED ↕
1	🗑	🔒		ECONOMICS	100	202,433	NOUN VERB ADJ ADV N+N ADJ+N	0 h

Step 6: Click *Noun* in the *Find keywords* table

FIND KEYWORDS ◉ SPECIFIC ○ FREQ
NOUN VERB ADJ ADV N+N ADJ+N

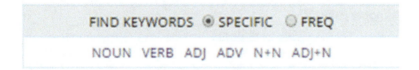

Step 7: View the noun keyword list

				SPECIFIC		ALL WIKIPEDIA	EXPECTED
HELP	WORD (CLICK TO SEE)	FREQ	# TEXTS	FREQ 45	10 TEXTS		
1	EXTERNALITY	55	15	1,669.9		301	0.0
2	MACROECONOMICS	52	21	359.7		1,321	0.1
3	GOOD	316	49	246.4		11,718	1.3
4	ELASTICITY	54	13	180.4		2,735	0.3
5	ECONOMIST	457	69	167.4		24,945	2.7
6	ECONOMICS	1378	88	154.4		81,569	8.9
7	MEAN	70	23	142.0		4,505	0.5
8	COMMODITY	115	23	114.3		9,198	1.0
9	WAGE	183	24	101.7		16,437	1.8
10	EQUILIBRIUM	158	28	96.4		14,986	1.6
11	PRICING	58	12	82.4		6,435	0.7
12	CAPITALISM	94	20	70.6		12,161	1.3
13	INCENTIVE	55	26	64.2		7,831	0.9
14	SAVING	47	13	52.9		8,112	0.9
15	ASSUMPTION	122	31	52.3		21,303	2.3

ECONOMICS (202,433 WORDS, 100 TEXTS) NOUN VERB ADJ ADV N+N ADJ+N   [ALL CORPORA] SAVE LIST

It is important to understand that these are not simply high-frequency words on the pages discussing economics. These are **keywords**. This means these words appear frequently in discussions of economics but also that they don't appear frequently on other pages on Wikipedia. Hence, they are key because they are unique to business communication. Instead of again just learning a general list of words, you have created a specialised list of vocabulary that is focused closely on your area of interest. This can help you be more strategic and efficient with your vocabulary study.

YOUR TURN 2.9

Create a specialised corpus and keyword list for an area in which you are interested. You could choose a hobby such as *surfing*, an issue about which you are concerned such as *climate change*, or your area of study such as *psychology*. Follow the same steps as above to create your corpus. List the top 10 keywords from your corpus.

Name of your specialised corpus: _____

Top 10 keywords

1. _____ 2. _____

3. _____ 4._____

5. _____ 6. _____

7. _____ 8. _____

9. _____ 10. _____

YOUR TURN 2.10

In this chapter, you completed many searches focused on vocabulary learning for academic purposes. Corpus searches can help us with more than academic vocabulary learning though. Choose a phrase such as *chill out, hang out, have a blast,* or perhaps a phrase you have recently heard at a coffee shop, the supermarket, or on campus. Search for the phrase in the corpus and report your findings. Answer questions such as:

1. Is the phrase used often?

   _____

2. In what situations (formal or informal) is the phrase likely used?

   _____

3. What does the phrase mean?

   _____

3 CORPUS SEARCHES FOR WRITING

IN THIS CHAPTER, you will complete a series of searches designed specifically for improving your writing skills. As a writing teacher, I have developed many of these searches for students in my own classes. Some of these searches were created to help a student correct an error or learn a new form while others were created to help students make better word choice decisions, find recent articles on a topic, or observe variation in the writing practices of different disciplines. The following searches will teach you how to use a corpus to help you revise an essay, correct grammar errors, make effective word choices, and guide register decisions. You will also learn how to use the News on the Web (NOW) Corpus to advance research projects on various topics. As with other chapters, we will begin with the COCA but use other corpora such as the Michigan Corpus of Upper-Level Student Papers (MICUSP), wordandphrase.info, Sketch Engine for Language Learning (SkELL), and the corpus-based FLAX Interactive Language Learning site.

Search 1: Starting sentences with conjunctions

You may have received a comment from a teacher on an essay that said, 'Don't start sentences with conjunctions.' Perhaps you wondered whether that was actually a general rule to follow or just the preference of this one instructor. A few quick corpus searches can help you answer your question and create a guideline to follow for your own writing. Let's complete searches for two frequently used conjunctions. Hopefully, the data will help us create our own guideline to follow for our own writing.

Step 1: In the COCA, click the *Chart* search function and enter . *And*

Tip 1: We want to view only results for the use of 'And' at the beginning of sentences, so you must enter a period in the search term and add one space between the punctuation and your search word. By doing this, you will get only sentences where 'And' follows a period; this will always be at the end of one sentence and the beginning of the next.

Tip 2: It's a good habit to click the Reset button before beginning new searches.

Step 2: Click *See frequency by section*

Step 3: View the results

SECTION (CLICK FOR SUB-SECTIONS) (SEE ALL SECTIONS AT ONCE)	FREQ	SIZE (M)	PER MIL	CLICK FOR CONTEXT (SEE ALL)
SPOKEN	506,110	109.4	4,626.59	
FICTION	114,018	104.9	1,086.91	
MAGAZINE	89,400	110.1	811.91	
NEWSPAPER	71,528	106.0	675.02	
ACADEMIC	25,605	103.4	247.58	
1990-1994	119,221	104.0	1,146.37	
1995-1999	151,209	103.4	1,461.70	
2000-2004	154,240	102.9	1,498.34	
2005-2009	162,378	102.0	1,591.30	
2010-2015	219,613	121.6	1,806.49	
TOTAL	1,613,322			SEE ALL TOKENS

The results are clear! The conjunction *and* is used frequently to start sentences in the spoken register but is much less frequent in the academic register. If we look at the PER MIL rate, it is clear that *and* has a rather lower use in university writing than in all the other registers. Let's see if another common conjunction follows the same pattern.

Step 4: Using the *Chart* search function, enter . *But* in the search bar

List Chart Collocates Compare KWIC

. But   [POS]

See frequency by section   Reset

☐ Sections Sort/Limit Options

Step 5: Click *See frequency by section*

Step 6: View the results

SECTION (CLICK FOR SUB-SECTIONS) (SEE ALL SECTIONS AT ONCE)	FREQ	SIZE (M)	PER MIL	CLICK FOR CONTEXT (SEE ALL)
SPOKEN	219,379	109.4	2,005.45	
FICTION	135,911	104.9	1,295.61	
MAGAZINE	142,989	110.1	1,298.59	
NEWSPAPER	119,607	106.0	1,128.75	
ACADEMIC	46,274	103.4	447.43	
1990-1994	114,335	104.0	1,099.38	
1995-1999	126,325	103.4	1,221.15	
2000-2004	130,311	102.9	1,265.88	
2005-2009	129,973	102.0	1,273.73	
2010-2015	163,216	121.6	1,342.58	
TOTAL	1,328,320			SEE ALL TOKENS

Is the same trend present for *but*? Actually, if you look at the PER MIL rate, you can see that *but* is used more frequently at the beginning of sentences than *and*. As discussed earlier, a corpus search does not simply give us a *yes* or *no* answer to our question, but it does give us information that can help us reach our own conclusions and create our own guidelines. It seems we could create a guideline for our writing about how to use conjunctions. The data has shown us that using conjunctions to start sentences is rare, so our guideline could be: avoid using conjunctions to start sentences. Perhaps it is acceptable to start sentences occasionally with conjunctions in our writing, but if we are writing a formal academic paper, it is likely best not to use them in that position frequently.

YOUR TURN 3.1

Try to think of other words or phrases which your teacher has commented are not appropriate for academic writing. Perhaps a teacher believes you are overusing a certain transition word or using a word that seems too informal for your project. Complete a search for the word or phrase, record your findings, and create a guideline on how you may use the word or phrase in future writing assignments.

Word/Phrase: _____

Findings:

_____

_____

_____

Guideline:

_____

_____

_____

Search 2: Phrasal verbs and academic writing

Writing teachers often make comments on student papers that say 'Too informal' or 'Be more academic'. While they may not be specific with their comments, it seems that often they are referring to the use of phrasal verbs in your academic writing. These are verbs such as *take down, find out, get up,* or *speed up.* There are so many phrasal verbs in English, but are they commonly used in the academic register or are they more common in spoken language?

Step 1: Click the *Chart* search function and enter *[figure] out* in the search bar

Tip: Use the [ ] so your data will include figure out, figures out, figured out, and figuring out.

List | **Chart** | Collocates Compare KWIC

[figure] out	[POS]
See frequency by section	Reset

☐ Sections Sort/Limit Options

Step 2: Click *See frequency by section* and view the results

SECTION (CLICK FOR SUB-SECTIONS) (SEE ALL SECTIONS AT ONCE)	FREQ	SIZE (M)	PER MIL	CLICK FOR CONTEXT (SEE ALL)
SPOKEN	7,341	109.4	67.11	
FICTION	5,332	104.9	50.83	
MAGAZINE	5,655	110.1	51.36	
NEWSPAPER	4,218	106.0	39.81	
ACADEMIC	1,244	103.4	12.03	
1990-1994	3,096	104.0	29.77	
1995-1999	3,954	103.4	38.22	
2000-2004	4,651	102.9	45.18	
2005-2009	5,355	102.0	52.48	
2010-2015	6,734	121.6	55.39	
TOTAL	47,580			SEE ALL TOKENS

It is clear that *figure out* is not commonly used in academic communication – only 12 times per 1 million words – and is much more frequent in the spoken register. This provides insight into the level of formality of a word or phrase. If a word is highly frequent in speaking but quite rare in academic writing, you can infer that the word is more informal and colloquial. If you should avoid using *figure out* in your formal writing, then what should you use? Let's search for several synonyms of *figure out*.

Step 3: Click the *Chart* search function and enter *[determine]* in the search bar

Step 4: Click *See frequency by section* and view the results

SECTION (CLICK FOR SUB-SECTIONS) (SEE ALL SECTIONS AT ONCE)	FREQ	SIZE (M)	PER MIL	CLICK FOR CONTEXT (SEE ALL)
SPOKEN	7,627	109.4	69.72	
FICTION	4,438	104.9	42.31	
MAGAZINE	12,417	110.1	112.77	
NEWSPAPER	10,328	106.0	97.47	
ACADEMIC	34,443	103.4	333.03	
1990-1994	13,483	104.0	129.65	
1995-1999	13,519	103.4	130.69	
2000-2004	13,359	102.9	129.77	
2005-2009	12,607	102.0	123.55	
2010-2015	16,285	121.6	133.96	
TOTAL	138,506			SEE ALL TOKENS

Step 5: Repeat the search with *[discover]*

SECTION (CLICK FOR SUB-SECTIONS) (SEE ALL SECTIONS AT ONCE)	FREQ	SIZE (M)	PER MIL	CLICK FOR CONTEXT (SEE ALL)
SPOKEN	7,153	109.4	65.39	
FICTION	9,924	104.9	94.60	
MAGAZINE	16,718	110.1	151.83	
NEWSPAPER	8,418	106.0	79.44	
ACADEMIC	10,395	103.4	100.51	
1990-1994	10,587	104.0	101.80	
1995-1999	10,219	103.4	98.78	
2000-2004	10,372	102.9	100.76	
2005-2009	9,930	102.0	97.31	
2010-2015	11,500	121.6	94.60	
TOTAL	105,216			SEE ALL TOKENS

Step 6: Repeat the search with *[observe]*

SECTION (CLICK FOR SUB-SECTIONS) (SEE ALL SECTIONS AT ONCE)	FREQ	SIZE (M)	PER MIL	CLICK FOR CONTEXT (SEE ALL)
SPOKEN	1,893	109.4	17.30	
FICTION	4,688	104.9	44.69	
MAGAZINE	10,296	110.1	93.51	
NEWSPAPER	3,313	106.0	31.27	
ACADEMIC	20,757	103.4	200.70	
1990-1994	8,490	104.0	81.64	
1995-1999	7,927	103.4	76.63	
2000-2004	7,474	102.9	72.60	
2005-2009	7,253	102.0	71.08	
2010-2015	9,803	121.6	80.64	
TOTAL	81,894			SEE ALL TOKENS

Although you must be careful to select the accurate synonym for your purpose, it seems rather clear that the one-word synonyms of *figure out* are more formal and, therefore, more appropriate for academic writing.

YOUR TURN 3.2

Test the previous observation that phrasal verbs are informal and less common in academic writing while their one-word synonyms are more formal and more frequent in this context. List 3 other common phrasal verbs and their one-word synonyms. Complete several *Chart* searches to determine whether the observation is accurate. Record the PER MIL rate rather than frequency.

	academic	spoken
phrasal verb 1: take off	1.73	10.02
2:		
3:		
4:		

	academic	spoken
One-word synonym 1: depart	3.84	1.55
2:		
3:		

Is the same pattern present?

_____

Create a guideline for your own language use:

_____

_____

_____

_____

Search 3: Signal words

A common signal word used in academic writing for introducing source material is *state*. In our academic writing, we may want to modify the signal word such as *state* to adjust how we report the information. For example, we may write, 'The author stated clearly . . .', 'The author stated emphatically . . .', or 'The author assertively stated . . .'. Let's do a search to discover the different ways speakers and writers modify the verb *state* and find other signal words that can be used to vary our word choice.

Step 1: Click *List* and enter *[state]* in the search bar

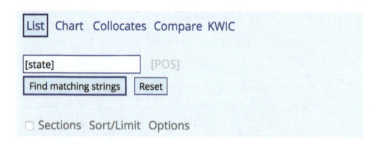

Step 2: Click the POS menu and select verb.ALL

Tip: Adding the verb.ALL tag will exclude uses of state *and* states *(for example, the state of New York, the United States) as nouns from our list.*

Step 3: Click the POS menu again and select adv.ALL

Your search bar should now have *[state]_v* _r**.

List Chart Collocates Compare KWIC

| [state]_v* _r* | adv.ALL | ⊟ |

Find matching strings   Reset

☐ Sections Sort/Limit Options

Step 4: Click *Find matching strings* and view results

		CONTEXT	FREQ	
1	◯	STATED EARLIER	193	
2	◯	STATED ABOVE	123	
3	◯	STATED CLEARLY	60	
4	◯	STATED PREVIOUSLY	60	
5	◯	STATES WHERE	60	
6	◯	STATED FLATLY	57	
7	◯	STATED PUBLICLY	53	
8	◯	STATED EXPLICITLY	49	
9	◯	STATE WHERE	46	
10	◯	STATE CLEARLY	44	
11	◯	STATED DIFFERENTLY	35	
12	◯	STATED SIMPLY	35	
13	◯	STATE HERE	34	
14	◯	STATED BEFORE	34	
15	◯	STATED REPEATEDLY	34	

Can you think of any weakness there may be in our search and the results? Notice in our results that there are only *[state]* + *adverb* patterns. However, it is possible that writers and speakers more frequently use *adverb* + *[state]* patterns. There are two ways we could resolve this error so that we reach the most accurate conclusion regarding adverb use with the signal verb *state*. First, we could do the same search but move the adverb POS tag to the position before *[state]* in the search bar. Second, we could do a *Collocates* search with the collocation window adjusted to 1L–1R and adv.ALL selected from the POS menu next to collocates. This second search would allow us to capture all the adverbs occurring one word to the left and one word to the right of *state*. As you complete searches, think carefully about different strategies for producing better results.

YOUR TURN 3.3

We completed a search for the verb form of *state* to determine the ways in which writers modify the verb. These adverbial modifiers allow writers to be more specific and detailed in their writing while making academic arguments. Learning the ways in which common academic words are used and commonly modified can be quite useful for your writing.

Complete a search for the noun form of *research* to determine which adjectives are often used to modify this important academic activity. Remember to close your collocation window to 1L–0R and select adj.ALL from the POS menu in order to focus only on the adjectives which appear before your search term.

Findings:

_____

_____

_____

_____

_____

Search 4: More with signal words

In your academic writing, it is important to vary your word choice rather than repeating the same few transition or signal words. If you continue your exploration of *state*, you can find synonyms that you could also use within your writing for introducing and integrating information and ideas from sources.

Step 1: Click *List* and enter *[=state]_v** in the search bar

Before you click *Find matching strings*, carefully look at the search syntax you entered in the search bar and answer the following questions:

1. Why use the brackets [ ] around *state*?
2. Why include the equals sign = before *state*?
3. Why add the POS tag *_v** after *state*?

As discussed, it is important to think carefully about the searches we perform and how we can complete searches that produce focused results. The more you can focus your searches, the more easily you will be able to answer your language questions and reach conclusions that guide your language use.

Were you able to answer the three questions? Let's consider them. First, by using the brackets [ ] around *state*, you are creating a lemma search so that your results will include the various verb forms from past and present verbs to progressives. Next, adding the equals sign = to your search will give you a list of synonyms of *state*. Because you are trying to expand your word choice, the synonym search is useful as it will yield results such as *maintain, maintaining, maintained* as well as *assert, asserted, asserting* that you might use in your essay. Finally, by adding the POS tag *v**, you make sure that only verbs are included in your results.

Step 2: Click *Sections*

Step 3: Select *Academic* in column 1 and *Spoken* in column 2

Tip: Select Frequency *next to the* Sorting *menu*

This option will allow you to compare synonyms of *state* when used in the spoken and academic registers. Thus, you will be able to choose a signal word that is appropriate for academic writing.

Step 4: Click *Find matching strings*

Step 5: View results

SEC 1 (ACADEMIC): 103,421,981 WORDS

	WORD/PHRASE	TOKENS 1	TOKENS 2	PM 1	PM 2	RATIO
1	SAY	22675	209020	219.2	1,910.7	0.1
2	STATE	10721	4044	103.7	37.0	2.8
3	MAINTAIN	10587	2962	102.4	27.1	3.8
4	EXPRESS	4785	2185	46.3	20.0	2.3
5	ASSERT	1944	317	18.8	2.9	6.5
6	DECLARE	1094	1121	10.6	10.2	1.0
7	AFFIRM	848	164	8.2	1.5	5.5
8	TESTIFY	560	2765	5.4	25.3	0.2
9	UTTER	141	78	1.4	0.7	1.9
10	AVER	29	0	0.3	0.0	28.0
11	AVOW	22	2	0.2	0.0	11.6

SEC 2 (SPOKEN): 109,391,643 WORDS

	WORD/PHRASE	TOKENS 2	TOKENS 1	PM 2	PM 1	RATIO
1	SAY	209020	22675	1,910.7	219.2	8.7
2	STATE	4044	10721	37.0	103.7	0.4
3	MAINTAIN	2962	10587	27.1	102.4	0.3
4	TESTIFY	2765	560	25.3	5.4	4.7
5	EXPRESS	2185	4785	20.0	46.3	0.4
6	DECLARE	1121	1094	10.2	10.6	1.0
7	ASSERT	317	1944	2.9	18.8	0.2
8	AFFIRM	164	848	1.5	8.2	0.2
9	UTTER	78	141	0.7	1.4	0.5
10	AVOW	2	22	0.0	0.2	0.1
11	AVER	0	29	0.0	0.3	0.0

In the table, the numbers in the column titled 'Tokens 1' represent frequency in the academic register while the 'Tokens 2' figures are for frequencies in the spoken register; the next two columns show corresponding per million rates. It is clear that *[say]* is the most common synonym of *state*, but it's also especially clear that *say* is much more typical of spoken communication; the per million rate for the academic register is only 219.2 but it is almost 2,000 for the spoken register! It is also clear that *maintain, express, assert,* and *affirm* are more appropriate options for academic communication.

YOUR TURN 3.4

Think of another word whose level of formality or informality you may not be sure about. Complete a search in which you compare its use in academic and spoken registers. Report your findings.

Word: _____

Findings:

_____

_____

_____

Search 5: Transition words

Writing teachers often stress the importance of transition words for moving a reader through your ideas and making your argument more comprehensible and coherent. Novice academic writers though sometimes are not sure which transition word (previously referred to as a linking adverbial) is most appropriate in a particular context or how to punctuate them correctly depending on their location in the sentence. Let's first look at the common transition word *however*.

Step 1: Select the *Chart* function and enter *however* in the search bar

List Chart Collocates Compare KWIC

however   [POS]

See frequency by section   Reset

☐ Sections Texts/Virtual Sort/Limit Options

Step 2: Click *See frequency by section*

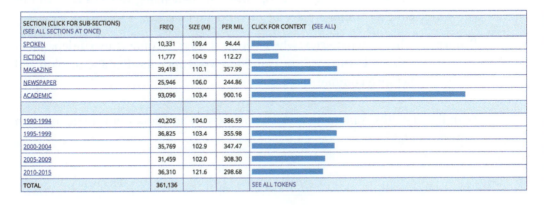

SECTION (CLICK FOR SUB-SECTIONS) (SEE ALL SECTIONS AT ONCE)	FREQ	SIZE (M)	PER MIL	CLICK FOR CONTEXT (SEE ALL)
SPOKEN	10,331	109.4	94.44	
FICTION	11,777	104.9	112.27	
MAGAZINE	39,418	110.1	357.99	
NEWSPAPER	25,946	106.0	244.86	
ACADEMIC	93,096	103.4	900.16	
1990-1994	40,205	104.0	386.59	
1995-1999	36,825	103.4	355.98	
2000-2004	35,769	102.9	347.47	
2005-2009	31,459	102.0	308.30	
2010-2015	36,310	121.6	298.68	
TOTAL	361,136			SEE ALL TOKENS

Woah! It's obvious that *however* is clearly most appropriate for the academic register. Yes, it's used in other registers, but it is clearly preferred in academic settings.

Step 3: Click on the bar next to *Academic* to view sample sentences using *however*

Step 4: Try to determine the three main punctuation patterns for *however* in the concordance lines

, it seems as if she has made the decision to leave this world. However, shortly after a final visit from her boyfriend Adam, Mia's perspective combines

with his housing project, do not solicit him for membership because of this. However, the conditions in which he lives create a story of gang life and hardship

and lunch, but the family did not receive monetary assistance from the government. However, they did receive nonmonetary assistance with finding and negotiating housing, paying bills,

students on the nature of scientific reasoning and communication " (p. 418). However, they also found that popular literature led to greater understanding of scientific concepts.

The content analysis revealed the potential of Twitter to engage students in scientific learning. However, much more research is needed to investigate the plausibility of following NASA's Twitter

A Book About Two Kids Counting Money is a children's book about math; however, when sharing it in the music classroom, street cries and clapping games emerge

soundscape prompted a municipal order in 1908 to suppress unnecessary noise in the city. However, the peddler's songs remained an important component of urban culture well into the

students develop self-expression. For example, the taiko drum sound is very powerful. However, general music teachers might not have access to, storage for, or experience

to self-express rhythmically within a taiko sound when the acoustic instrument is not accessible. However, virtual instruments encourage fine motor tapping movement, rather than gross motor striking

requiring students to think deeply about music making and music meaning. It is, however, challenging to focus on and document student thinking that extends beyond skill development.Drawing on

thinking dispositions as a guide when planning large units of study. There are, however, several thinking routines that can energize daily classroom activities. In the Elaboration Game

point, I have focused on listening and describing music. These ideas do, however, have direct application to music making. When our students are actively engaged in

and sounds of African musics is an invaluable addition to any multicultural music curriculum. However, many lesson plans, books, and articles about African musics often focus purely

of the learner is defined commonly by ethnicity, economic conditions, and gender; however, there are other issues of diversity—such as the visual or auditory abilities or the

one's own emotional strengths. # These intelligences are found in all people; however, each person usually excels in only one or two. If teachers can determine

different intelligences, and 44% had used MI to some extent in their teaching. However, less than 1% indicated they followed MI theory closely or used it consistently in

guide instruction, develop the budget, and lead the charge for student success. However, one need not look far to realize that this concept in its purest form

Pattern 1: From reading the concordance lines, it seems that the most common way *however* is used is at the beginning of the sentence followed by a comma. For example, 'However, they did receive . . .'.

Pattern 2: You can also see that *however* is often inserted into the independent clause. For example, 'It is, however, challenging to focus . . .'. In this case, a comma is place before and after *however.*

Pattern 3: The third pattern is when *however* is used to connect two independent clauses. In this case, the transition word appears after a semicolon and before a comma.

Scan the first 30 sample sentences on your screen and count how many of each pattern you find.

	Frequency
Pattern 1: at the beginning of a sentence	
Pattern 2: within an independent clause	
Pattern 3: to join two independent clauses	

YOUR TURN 3.5

Think of another word whose use and proper punctuation is confusing and challenging. For example, some students make errors punctuating dependent clauses that begin with subordinate conjunctions such as *when*, *while*, *although*, and *because*. Complete a search for your chosen word and summarise your findings.

Word: _____

Findings:

_____

_____

_____

Search 6: *KWIC* searches and grammatical patterns in SkELL

It is possible that some of the sample sentences resulting from searches in the COCA are difficult to understand. If that is the case, you may prefer a corpus created specifically for English language learners called Sketch Engine for Language Learning (SkELL). While it does not offer as many of the functions and capabilities as the COCA and other corpora we have used, it does provide simplified output that may in some situations be more useful for you.

Step 1: Go to SkELL at http://skell.sketchengine.co.uk/run.cgi/skell

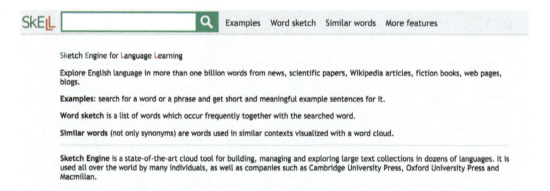

Step 2: Enter the frequent academic word *significant* in the search bar

In the area next to the search bar, you will see the SkELL functions: *Examples, Word sketch, Similar words.*

Step 3: Click *Examples*

significant   136.88 hits per million

1   A second **significant** issue is climate change .

2   A **significant** tax differential does still exist however .

3   HB 8 makes three **significant** changes regarding probation eligibility .

4   The policy has already achieved **significant** outcomes .

5   Neither bourgeoisie nor working class was **significant** .

6   Region trusts are lastly travelled existing various illness **significant** areas .

7   To achieve such internal integrity usually requires **significant** restructuring efforts .

8   No **significant** mortality difference between decks was observed .

9   But major structural changes require **significant** resources .

10   Her typical clients were **significant** corporations doing international business .

11   The high growth firms literature has three **significant** weaknesses .

12   International surety bond underwriting presents **significant** obstacles .

13   That voltage drop generates **significant** unwanted heat .

14   **Significant** differences were found between recall conditions .

15   A business marketing strategy requires conducting **significant** marketing research .

It is clear from the sentences listed that SkELL provides simpler sentences. It might be that these simpler sentences will help you better focus on how the word is used and will help you make better choices about how to use the word in your writing.

Step 4: Click *Word sketch*

This option provides some rather useful information. You can see that SkELL provides lists of nouns commonly modified by the adjective *significant* such as *difference* and *finding*, common adverbial modifiers such as *statistically*, *clinically*, and *historically*, as well as the verbs with which it often appears. SkELL provides collocation information in a format which you might feel is more user-friendly.

Step 5: Click *Similar words*

For the final SkELL search option, the results display words which are similar to *significant*. It is important to understand though that the words in the word cloud are not all synonyms of your search word. The cloud does include synonyms (for example, *important*) but it also includes words that are used in similar contexts (for example, *possible*).

YOUR TURN 3.6

Complete two additional searches using SkELL for other words which you often encounter in academic settings. Summarise your findings.

Findings:

_____

_____

_____

_____

_____

Tip: If you can't think of an academic word to search for in SkELL, visit the Academic Word List website at http://www.uefap.com/vocab/select/awl.htm.

Search 7: Strengthening word choice with the FLAX Corpus

Another rather user-friendly corpus resource for improving your writing is the FLAX Corpus. This site is focused on helping you see common collocates of your search word and allows you to search either a corpus of 3 million Wikipedia articles, the 100 million word British National Corpus (BNC), or the British Academic Written English Corpus (BAWE) of 2,500 university student essays. To access the FLAX Corpus resource, search *FLAX collocations*; the site will be the first result in Google.

Step 1: Open the FLAX site

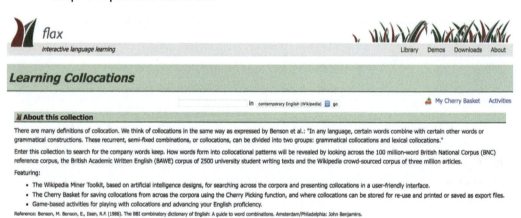

On the homepage, you will notice the bar for entering your search word in the middle screen. Next to the search bar, there is a drop-down menu from which you can choose the corpus you would like to use for your query.

Step 2: Enter *discover* in the search bar

Learning Collocations

My Cherry Basket   Activities

discover   in contemporary English (Wikipedia) go

Step 3: Select *academic English (BAWE)* from the menu

Learning Collocations

My Cherry Basket   Activities

discover   in academic English (BAWE) go

Step 4: Click *go*

Step 5: View results

discover + noun	discover the truth	12	discover the extent of	6
	discover the cause of	9	discover the delights of	5
	discover the identity of	8	discover the reasons for	5
	discover the source of	6	discover things	5
	discover ways of	6	discover the extent to	5
				>>> more
noun + to + discover	attempt to discover	19	surprise to discover	7
	way to discover	11	chance to discover	5
	desire to discover	9	shock to discover	5
	opportunity to discover	9	survey to discover	4
	time to discover	7	investigation to discover	4
				>>> more
adjective + to + discover	surprised to discover	34	delighted to discover	10
	able to discover	29	horrified to discover	9
	possible to discover	15	easy to discover	8
	difficult to discover	15	unable to discover	7
	shocked to discover	11	pleased to discover	6
				>>> more
verb + to + discover	trying to discover	26	beginning to discover	6
	need to discover	14	aims to discover	6
	attempting to discover	7	designed to discover	6
	seek to discover	7	wanted to discover	6
	failed to discover	7	like to discover	5
				>>> more

Step 6: Click on one of the sample patterns to view concordance lines

19	🍒	surprise to **discover**		7

- It had come as quite a **surprise to discover** he was charming, very generous, and enormous fun to be with.
- It usually comes as a **surprise to discover** how angry the patient is, because superficially and consciously he blames but himself.
- It came as no great **surprise to discover** that, in the Department's view, the new Committee could well function within the structure of the Technician Education Council.
- It was like stepping from the main street into a cobbled alley's curiosity shop that shock of **surprise to discover** again what an intricate and peculiar organ the imagination is, what extravagant uses it has found for time.
- It has often been a **surprise to discover** the presence of an extensive spread of buildings well beyond the enclosure, this lack of awareness has led occasionally to their discovery all too late, whilst they were being ravaged by development.
- It is no **surprise to discover** its presence, since it must surely belong to a very early stage in the mental development of the human species; indeed it represents one aspect of the principle of treating like as like, it can be seen as common perceptual property for all sentient organisms.
- It will come as no **surprise to discover**, then, that Spencer was highly critical of statutory intervention, arguing that it stifled liberty and led to rigidity and uniformity: Society, a living growing organism, placed within apparatuses of dead, rigid, mechanical formulas, can not fail to be hampered and pinched.

Step 7: Click on one of the *family words* listed above the results

The results in the image below display patterns of the noun *discoveries*.

used as a noun

adjective + discoveries					
	🍒 new **discoveries**	47	🍒 exciting **discoveries**	7	
	🍒 recent **discoveries**	18	🍒 further **discoveries**	6	
	🍒 important **discoveries**	12	🍒 major **discoveries**	6	
	🍒 scientific **discoveries**	11	🍒 latest **discoveries**	5	
	🍒 significant **discoveries**	9	🍒 great **discoveries**	5	
				>>> more	

discoveries + of + noun					
	🍒 **discoveries** of science	5	🍒 **discoveries** of hitherto unknown kinds	1	
	🍒 **discoveries** of the century	3	🍒 **discoveries** of articulated thelodonts	1	
	🍒 number of **discoveries**	3	🍒 **discoveries** of these new animals	1	
	🍒 importance of these **discoveries**	2	🍒 **discoveries** of esoteric viruses	1	
	🍒 history of **discoveries**	2	🍒 **discoveries** of atomic physics	1	
				>>> more	

discoveries + preposition + noun					
	🍒 **discoveries** in this field	2	🍒 **discoveries** in medicine	1	
	🍒 way for later testable **discoveries**	1	🍒 **discoveries** like the superconducting buckminsterfullerenes	1	
	🍒 groundwork for endless **discoveries**	1	🍒 **discoveries** during their careers	1	
	🍒 **discoveries** to his credit	1	🍒 **discoveries** from his study	1	
	🍒 **discoveries** to chance	1	🍒 **discoveries** at their reception	1	
				>>> more	

verb + discoveries					
	🍒 utilising her **discoveries**	2	🍒 make similar **discoveries** in	1	
	🍒 making new **discoveries**	2	🍒 include smaller adjacent **discoveries** in	1	
	🍒 containing gas **discoveries**	2	🍒 announced large new **discoveries** in	1	
	🍒 make these **discoveries** represents	1	🍒 illustrate his growing **discoveries** in	1	
	🍒 make scientific **discoveries** actually work	1	🍒 made good **discoveries** near	1	
				>>> more	

Similar to the SkELL search completed in search 6, the interface for FLAX is intended for language learners and is rather user-friendly. This may make it a more useful resource for you initially, but you should remember that more comprehensive information about your search word is produced by the COCA and wordandphrase.info. Nonetheless, the information FLAX provides can certainly be useful for you as you write and revise an essay. In the results, you are able to view the various patterns in which *discover* appears such as *adjective* + *to* + *discover*, *verb* + *to* + *discover*, and *noun* + *to* + *discover*. These structures and the supporting examples can help you craft more effective sentences but also revise and test sentences which you have already written. Hopefully, when your instructor next comments 'Odd phrasing' or 'Awkward wording', you can go to FLAX and investigate why your instructor made this comment and how you can revise the structure in the next draft of your essay.

YOUR TURN 3.7

Explore FLAX and investigate an academic word of your own choice.

Word: _____

Common grammatical patterns:
_____, _____, _____

Most frequently used phrase:

_____

Search 8: Using the NOW Corpus for research

University students are regularly assigned research projects by teachers in a variety of their university courses. It is possible that you will be asked to investigate a current topic with which you may not be familiar. While all of our searches thus far have primarily focused on using corpora for language learning, it is also possible to use a corpus to help you get started on a research project. In the initial stage when you are learning about an issue and trying to understand the different viewpoints people have towards the topic, using a corpus can be a useful tool. For this search, you'll use the NOW Corpus. This corpus is perfect for this task because it is updated with 4–5 million words daily; actually, you would not be able to find the information we are seeking in most corpora. However, if you're looking for recent newspaper and magazine articles discussing a topic, the NOW Corpus can provide you with many sources. Furthermore, if you see an article that may be useful for your project, the NOW Corpus allows you to click the link and go directly to the article and the website where it was posted. In this search, we are going to search for the term *pipeline*. In recent environmental debates in North America, there have been strong debates about whether to build several large oil pipelines. If you were asked to write a paper about one of these debates or another current controversial topic, the NOW Corpus would be a great resource to use.

Step 1: Go to https://corpus.byu.edu and enter the News on the Web (NOW) Corpus

English	# words	language/dialect	time period	compare
News on the Web (NOW)	4.6 billion+	20 countries / Web	2010-yesterday	
Global Web-Based English (GloWbE)	1.9 billion	20 countries / Web	2012-13	
Wikipedia Corpus	1.9 billion	English	-2014	Info
Hansard Corpus (British Parliament)	1.6 billion	British	1803-2005	Info
Corpus of Contemporary American English (COCA)	520 million	American	1990-2015	★ ★ ★ ★ ★
Corpus of Historical American English (COHA)	400 million	American	1810-2009	★ ★
Corpus of US Supreme Court Opinions	130 million	American	1790s-present	
TIME Magazine Corpus	100 million	American	1923-2006	
Corpus of American Soap Operas	100 million	American	2001-2012	★
British National Corpus (BYU-BNC)*	100 million	British	1980s-1993	★ ★
Strathy Corpus (Canada)	50 million	Canadian	1970s-2000s	
CORE Corpus	50 million	Web registers	-2014	

Step 2: Click *Collocates*, enter *pipeline* in the search bar, and set the
collocation window at 4L–0R

We are setting the collocation window at 4L–0R because we want to find articles
about specific pipeline projects in the news.

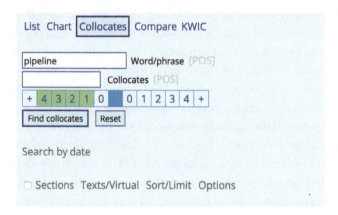

Step 3: Click *Find collocates*

Remember that the NOW Corpus is updated daily, so the results displayed in
these images will differ from the results you produce in your search.

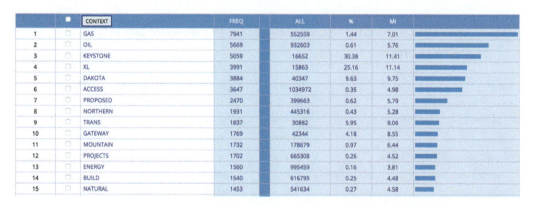

		CONTEXT	FREQ	ALL	%	MI	
1		GAS	7941	552559	1.44	7.01	
2		OIL	5669	932603	0.61	5.76	
3		KEYSTONE	5059	16652	30.38	11.41	
4		XL	3991	15863	25.16	11.14	
5		DAKOTA	3884	40347	9.63	9.75	
6		ACCESS	3647	1034972	0.35	4.98	
7		PROPOSED	2470	399663	0.62	5.79	
8		NORTHERN	1931	445316	0.43	5.28	
9		TRANS	1837	30882	5.95	9.06	
10		GATEWAY	1769	42344	4.18	8.55	
11		MOUNTAIN	1732	178679	0.97	6.44	
12		PROJECTS	1702	665308	0.26	4.52	
13		ENERGY	1560	995459	0.16	3.81	
14		BUILD	1540	616795	0.25	4.48	
15		NATURAL	1453	541634	0.27	4.58	

In the list, you can see the names of several recent pipeline debates. For example,
on the list are the proposed Keystone XL Pipeline and the Dakota Access
Pipeline.

Step 4: Click *Dakota*, the location of one of the most controversial pipeline projects in the United States

1	18-04-23 NZ	New Zealand Herald	A B C	who suffered a serious arm injury in an explosion while protesting the Dakota Access oil pipeline in North Dakota. # Prosecutors contend authorities properly
2	18-04-06 US	WHEC	A B C	# BISMARCK, N.D. (AP) -- The developer of the Dakota Access oil pipeline that goes under a reservoir in the Dakotas has submitted a court-ordered spill respon
3	18-04-03 NZ	New Zealand Herald	A B C	Earth First can be sued as an established group for opposing the Dakota Access oil pipeline, an attorney with the Center for Constitutional Rights says. # Pame
4	18-03-30 NZ	New Zealand Herald	A B C	in its argument that it can't be sued for opposing the Dakota Access oil pipeline. # The Center for Constitutional Rights maintains Earth First is an unstructured
5	18-03-25 US	HuffPost	A B C	, where indigenous activists and environmentalists were protesting the construction of the Dakota Access oil pipeline through a sacred water source. # " I foun
6	18-03-20 NZ	New Zealand Herald	A B C	More time is needed to finish additional court-ordered environmental study of the Dakota Access oil pipeline due to difficulties in getting needed information f
7	18-03-08 US	WQAD.com	A B C	officials of being uncooperative as they conduct a court-ordered study of the Dakota Access oil pipeline's impact on tribal water supply. # The Standing Rock Si
8	18-03-07 NZ	New Zealand Herald	A B C	) -- The American Indian tribe leading the legal fight against the Dakota Access oil pipeline is accusing federal officials of being uncooperative as they complete
9	18-03-04 CA	CBC.ca	A B C	almost 800,000 litres of oil spilled from the Keystone pipeline in South Dakota, a pipeline less than a decade old. # One of these spills was among the largest
10	18-02-18 US	Arizona Daily Star	A B C	another alum's long account of his daughter going to North Dakota to protest the pipeline, and she's not even an alumna. # What do you think I

The results display a list of the most recent articles that have discussed this particular topic. On the list, you can see articles listed from websites around the world.

Step 5: Click on a source to go to the webpage for the article

BUSINESS

Tribes fighting pipeline drop appeal but battle continues

20 May, 2017 1:25am   ⊙ 2 minutes to read

AP

BISMARCK, N.D. (AP) " American Indian tribes who are still fighting the Dakota Access oil pipeline in court have dropped an appeal of a federal judge's decision that allowed final construction to proceed on the project that is just two weeks from operating commercially.

U.S. District Judge James Boasberg in early March refused to stop completion of the pipeline based on the claims of Sioux tribes that it threatens water they consider sacred. The Cheyenne River Sioux appealed the decision to the U.S. Court of Appeals for the District of Columbia Circuit, which refused to grant an emergency order stopping oil from flowing while the appeal was decided.

Developer Energy Transfer Partners finished construction on the pipeline and began filling it with oil in late March. Spokeswoman Vicki Granado confirmed this week that the line fill process has been completed.

"Our commercial operations begin June 1, whereby we will begin transporting crude per our contracts with shippers," she said.

As you can see, the NOW Corpus will link you directly to the webpage where you may read the full article. Instead of doing a general Google search to collect background information, a NOW Corpus search provides a more focused list of potential sources for your project. Whether you are doing a research project on endangered wolves, climate change, a particular city, or many more, the NOW Corpus is great place to get started.

YOUR TURN 3.8

Using the NOW Corpus, search for a keyword that has been used often within a recent controversial debate or within in area in which you are interested. List the word or words you chose to search and discuss whether you were able to find quality articles on your topic.

Word(s): _____

Findings:

_____

_____

_____

Search 9: Understanding disciplinary differences with the MICUSP

For this search, we will use another unique online corpus: the Michigan Corpus of Upper-Level Student Papers (MICUSP). The MICUSP contains over 800 essays written by upper-level (undergraduate seniors and 1st, 2nd, and 3rd year graduate students) from a variety of academic disciplines such as Biology, Mechanical Engineering, Psychology, and many more. You can focus your searches by particular textual features (abstracts, discussion of results, methodology, and so on) and paper types (argumentative essay, proposal, report, and so on). Thus, if you are writing a particular paper type within a certain discipline, you can access quite specific language information to help guide you.

For this search, we will investigate variation in the use of modal verbs across academic disciplines. These words, such as *may*, *could*, and *might*, are called **hedges** because they reduce the strength of a claim or argument. Rather than presenting an idea or information as 100 per cent truth, you can use a hedge to reduce the power of the statement. In contrast, the modal *will* is called a **booster** because it more assertively presents a claim or argument.

Step 1: Open the MICUSP at http://micusp.elicorpora.info/

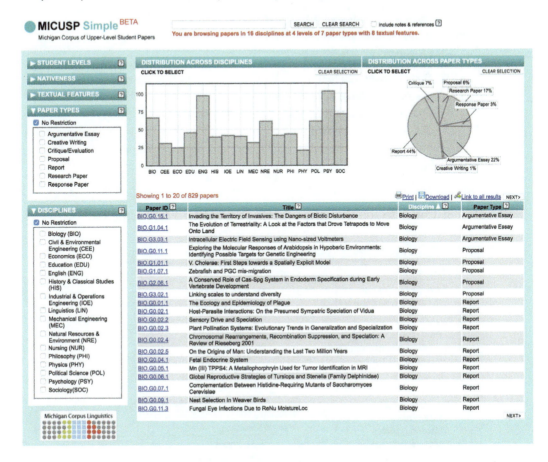

Review the options in the left bar of the homepage. First, you will see options to select by student level (undergraduate or 1st, 2nd, or 3rd year graduate), native-ness (Native English Speaker or Non-native English Speaker), textual features, paper types, and disciplines. For our search, let's focus on undergraduate writing and their use of hedges and boosters.

Step 2: Click *Senior Undergrad* for student levels

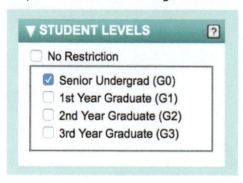

Step 3: Check to see the other options are marked *No Restriction*

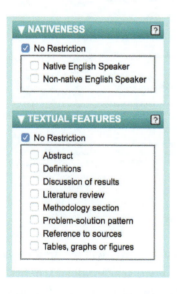

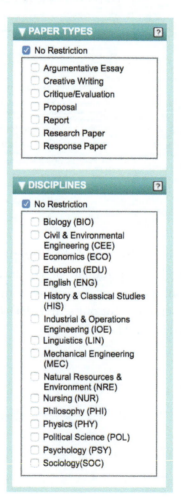

Step 4: Enter *might* in the search bar and click *Search*

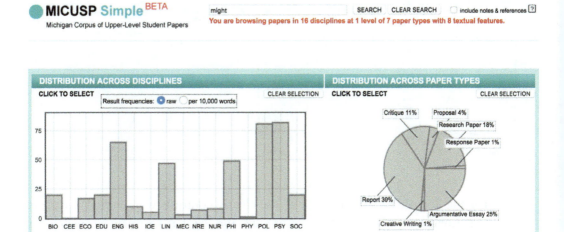

Interestingly, the hedge *might* is used most frequently in social science disciplines such as English, Linguistics, Political Science, and Psychology but rather infrequently in the sciences. It may be possible to speculate that claims and arguments in social sciences are presented more cautiously and carefully and that strong claims are less frequent but also less appropriate.

Step 5: Enter *will* in the search bar and click *Search*

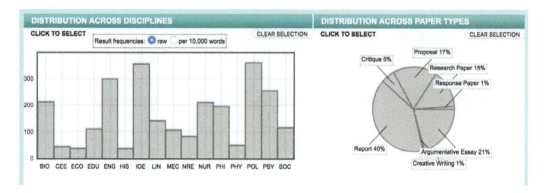

For the booster *will*, the pattern of use clearly contrasts with *might*. We can see that English and Political Science use *will* and *might* at a similar frequency, but Industrial & Operations Engineering, which had only 5 instances of *might*, has over 350 instances of *will*. Again, this may help us guide our writing as we better understand the values of various disciplines and the level of strength with which we should present a claim.

YOUR TURN 3.9

In previous searches, we have investigated the use of transition words such as *however*. It could be useful though to look at example sentences of transition words from student papers.

Search for the transition word *however* and two others in the MICUSP. Report your findings.

Transitions: however, _____, _____

Findings:

_____

_____

_____

4 CORPUS SEARCHES FOR CULTURAL STUDY AND CONVERSATION TOPICS

THE SEARCHES IN this chapter are not designed to help you revise an essay, expand your vocabulary, or learn a new grammar structure. Instead, the searches in Chapter 4 are intended to be provocative, to spark your thinking, and reveal insights into the cultures that these corpora represent and reflect. These searches will hopefully lead to discussion amongst your friends and classmates and push you to ask additional questions and reflect upon your findings. This chapter will also help you learn to identify and interpret patterns in language use as you continue to develop your ability to conduct corpus analysis.

For teachers, you can implement these searches or design similar ones to promote conversation in your speaking classes.

Search 1: *Teenagers, Zombies,* and *Selfies*

As you have seen in previous chapters, there are many practical uses of corpora. Yes, a corpus search can help you learn academic vocabulary or revise an essay, but corpus searches can also reveal some rather exciting and intriguing cultural insights. One example of this is to track the life cycle of a word. It can be interesting and indeed fun to learn when a word was first used and how its use has evolved over time. For these searches, we will use the Google Ngram Viewer (a billion word web corpus based on Google Books), the Corpus of Historical American English (COHA, a 400 million word corpus compiled of texts from 1810–2009), and the NOW Corpus we explored in Chapter 3. First, we'll use the Google Ngram Viewer, a massive corpus but without many of the options of the COCA and other resources we've explored. It's great for tracking trends over time. Let's look at a few examples.

Step 1: Open the Google Ngram Viewer at https://books.google.com/ngrams

Step 2: Enter *teenager* and *teenagers* in the search bar

Step 3: Click *Search lots of books* and view results

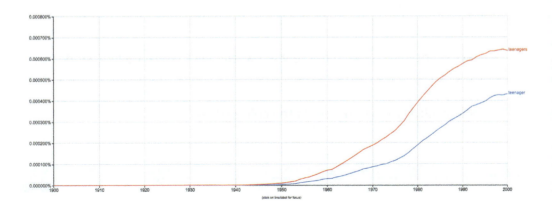

Interesting! Why prior to 1940 are there no uses of the word *teenager*? What is happening in the world that suddenly a new word and a new label for a group of individuals has become necessary? You may speculate that in the period following World War II, society and culture were experiencing tremendous changes. In post-war USA, famous writers such as Jack Kerouac and the Beat Generation were writing about a new sort of freedom and independence, and young people were becoming more independent and more mobile than ever before. It's rather fascinating that this cultural shift is displayed in language use.

Step 4: Go to https://corpus.byu.edu and open the Corpus of Historical
American English (COHA)

Step 5: Enter *teenager* in the search bar and click *Find matching strings*

Step 6: Click on the number in the column '1940'

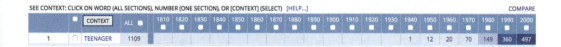

After clicking the number, you will be able to view the first corpus-attested sample of the use of *teenager*. In contrast to the Google Ngram Viewer, the COHA allows you to see the exact sentence and paragraph in which the word was used and the source in which it appeared. Interestingly, *teenager* is first recorded in a discussion about parents and how they should deal with their teen's use of the family car. Also, you can notice that only the masculine pronoun *he* is used. Does this mean that a female teenager at the time was neither allowed nor expected to be able to operate the family car? Again, some rather interesting insights about the culture of this period. Let's try another one.

Step 7: Return to the Google Ngram Viewer

Step 8 Enter *zombie* and *zombies* in the bar and click *Search lots of books*

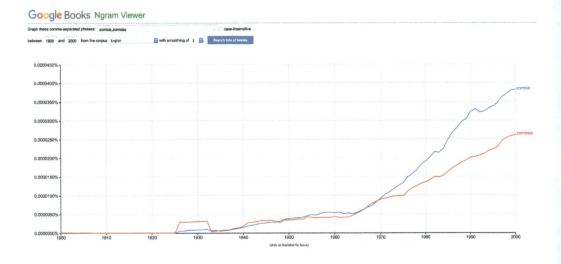

Step 9: Return to the COHA

Step 10: Enter zombie in the search bar and click *Find matching strings*

When is the first recorded example of *zombie*? Where was the term used and what was it describing? Interestingly, the use of the term declines for a period and then increases in the middle of the century. Does this reveal anything about American culture? Some have argued that the zombie symbolises greed, consumerism, and obsession with money and profits.

Step 11: Go to the NOW Corpus

Step 12: Click *Chart*

Step 13: Enter *selfie* in the search bar and click *See frequency by section*

List Chart Collocates Compare KWIC

selfie   [POS]
See frequency by section   Reset

Search by date

☐ Sections Texts/Virtual Sort/Limit Options

Step 14: View results

Frequency by year   (See frequency by country)

SECTION (CLICK FOR SUB-SECTIONS) (SEE ALL SECTIONS AT ONCE)	FREQ	SIZE (M)	PER MIL	CLICK FOR CONTEXT (SEE ALL)
2010-A	6	115.2	0.05	
2010-B	3	129.2	0.02	
2011-A	37	145.1	0.26	
2011-B	8	160.0	0.05	
2012-A	186	185.1	1.00	
2012-B	20	186.4	0.11	
2013-A	349	196.9	1.77	
2013-B	1,537	204.9	7.50	
2014-A	2,259	209.8	10.76	
2014-B	2,822	219.9	12.83	
2015-A	3,004	223.8	13.42	
2015-B	3,406	289.1	11.78	
2016-A	5,827	684.5	8.51	
2016-B	6,549	853.8	7.67	
2017-A	6,190	847.6	7.30	
TOTAL	32,203			SEE ALL TOKENS

In what year was the first sample recorded in the corpus? Read the sample sentences from that year. Do you notice anything interesting?

YOUR TURN 4.1

Think of a word such as *teenager* or *selfie* that may offer some cultural insights.
Complete a series of searches and see what you discover.

Word: _____

Date of first use:

_____

Interesting trends:

_____

Other findings:

_____

Search 2: What happened to *global warming*?

In 2006, when Al Gore released the now famous documentary *An Inconvenient Truth: A Global Warning,* he used the phrase *global warming* approximately 10 times in the film but never once did he use the now common term *climate change*. It now seems that *climate change* is the most frequently used term and that instances of *global warming* seem increasingly uncommon. Why would our choice between global warming and climate change adjust over time? Is the switch meaningful and important? Let's go to the corpus and investigate these patterns.

Step 1: Open the COCA

Step 2: Choose the *Chart* search, enter *global warming* in the search bar, and click *See frequency by section*

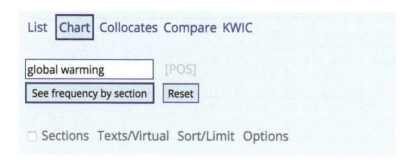

Step 3: View the results and make a note of trends in how the term is used over time

1990-1994		710	104.0	6.83	
1995-1999		542	103.4	5.24	
2000-2004		1,025	102.9	9.96	
2005-2009		2,194	102.0	21.50	
2010-2015		1,270	121.6	10.45	
TOTAL		11,482			SEE ALL TOKENS

Step 4: Click on 2005–2009 to look more carefully at those years

SECTION	FREQ	SIZE (M)	PER MIL	CLICK FOR CONTEXT
2005	258	20.8	12.42	
2006	449	20.8	21.61	
2007	611	20.3	30.04	
2008	478	20.1	23.84	
2009	398	20.1	19.81	

Step 5: Complete the same search process for *climate change*

1990-1994	340	104.0	3.27	
1995-1999	822	103.4	7.95	
2000-2004	1,030	102.9	10.01	
2005-2009	2,331	102.0	22.84	
2010-2015	4,033	121.6	33.17	
TOTAL	17,112			SEE ALL TOKENS

Take a moment and think about why this change in use of the two terms possibly occurred. Do you have an answer? No? Think about this: does one of the phrases possibly create a more fearful and scary view of the world and the change it is experiencing? Some people argue that this change was intentional and purposeful because *global warming* inspires a more ominous and frightening view of the future. In contrast, *climate* may make us think of breezy spring days and *change* as a natural process. Thus, some people believe that there was an effort to promote the use of *climate change* because it seemed less dangerous and frightening. Interesting!

Remember that the effectiveness of your search and the quality of your findings is influenced by the corpus you choose. If you had chosen the Google Ngram Viewer to complete the search, you would only be able to view data until the year 2000. Also, you may want to compare the American use with the British use by using the BNC, but the BNC only includes texts until 1993. You could choose to use the NOW Corpus, but then you would lose samples from before 2010. Before you start your searches, always first consider which corpus is most appropriate to answer your particular question.

YOUR TURN 4.2

Track another word or phrase whose frequency or meaning has likely changed recently. For example, you could explore a set of terms such as *vegetarian* and *vegan*.

1. How has the frequency of the word(s) changed over time?

_____

2. What do you think influenced this change?

_____

_____

Search 3:   Are different adjectives used when modifying *man* and *woman*?

We have completed searches that investigated various words and phrases and how their use has changed over time. For this search, you will explore the adjectives which are most commonly used to describe *man* and *woman*. Do you think the adjectives most frequently used to modify *man* and *woman* are different or quite similar? If the adjective collocates of these two words were indeed distinct, what might these differences indicate about society? Before we complete the searches, first think about which adjectives most frequently appear with the nouns *man* and *woman*. It will be interesting to again assess whether our intuitions about language use are either confirmed or refuted by the corpus data.

Step 1:   Complete the chart with the top 5 adjectives you feel are most frequently used with *man* and *woman*

man	woman
1.	1.
2.	2.
3.	3.
4.	4.
5.	5.

Step 2: In the COCA, click *Compare* and enter *man* and *woman* in the
search bar

List Chart Collocates Compare KWIC
man	Word1 [POS]
woman	Word2 [POS]
Collocates [POS]
+ 4 3 2 1 0 0 1 2 3 4 +
Compare words   Reset
☐ Sections Texts/Virtual Sort/Limit Options

Step 3: Click adj.ALL in the drop-down menu next to Collocates

List Chart Collocates Compare KWIC
man	Word1 [POS]
woman	Word2 [POS]
_j*	Collocates adj.ALL ⊟
+ 4 3 2 1 0 0 1 2 3 4 +
Compare words   Reset

By placing the adj.ALL tag in the Collocates bar, you are able to focus your
results on descriptive adjectives and can prevent other parts of speech from
appearing.

Step 4: Adjust the collocation window at 2L–2R and click *Compare words*

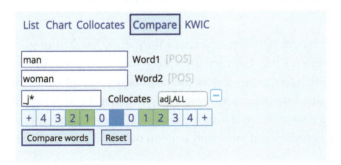

By setting the collocation at 2L–2R, your results will capture the attributive adjectives used before the noun (the *tall* man) as well as the predicative adjectives (the man is *tall*) used after the noun and a linking verb (*am, is, are, was, were*).

Step 5: View results

SORTED BY FREQUENCY: CHANGE TO RATIO

WORD 1 (W1): MAN (1.87)

	WORD	W1	W2	W1/W2	SCORE
1	YOUNG	15958	9068	1.8	0.9
2	UNIDENTIFIED	14560	11063	1.3	0.7
3	OLD	14482	4598	3.1	1.7
4	BLACK	3891	2191	1.8	0.9
5	WHITE	3288	1212	2.7	1.5
6	GOOD	2508	512	4.9	2.6
7	BIG	2168	203	10.7	5.7
8	DEAD	2070	415	5.0	2.7
9	OTHER	1665	1318	1.3	0.7
10	OLDER	1657	1250	1.3	0.7
11	LITTLE	1403	271	5.2	2.8
12	GREAT	1278	174	7.3	3.9
13	TALL	1136	326	3.5	1.9
14	POOR	1015	426	2.4	1.3
15	BEST	870	67	13.0	6.9

WORD 2 (W2): WOMAN (0.53)

	WORD	W2	W1	W2/W1	SCORE
1	UNIDENTIFIED	11063	14560	0.8	1.4
2	YOUNG	9068	15958	0.6	1.1
3	OLD	4598	14482	0.3	0.6
4	BLACK	2191	3891	0.6	1.1
5	BEAUTIFUL	1703	164	10.4	19.4
6	OTHER	1318	1665	0.8	1.5
7	OLDER	1250	1657	0.8	1.4
8	WHITE	1212	3288	0.4	0.7
9	PREGNANT	814	7	116.3	217.4
10	AMERICAN	801	373	2.1	4.0
11	ONLY	762	856	0.9	1.7
12	ELDERLY	750	633	1.2	2.2
13	RIGHT	577	628	0.9	1.7
14	GOOD	512	2508	0.2	0.4
15	PRETTY	509	15	33.9	63.4

We have seen this type of *Compare* output before, but it is important to understand the data displayed in the output. In this output, the words are listed by their frequency. For example, in the left output panel, *good* is listed sixth because its frequency is the sixth most commonly used adjective with the noun *man*. What do these colours mean though? The colour bands reflect the degree of difference in the frequency of the two words. For instance, the difference in use of *old* or *unidentified* is not as significant as the difference between *big* or *best*. In this search, the data is sorted by frequency, but it is also possible to sort by ratio. You can click 'CHANGE TO RATIO' at the top of the screen to rank the lists by ratio. We will sort by ratio in the next search.

Search 4: Possession and the possessives *his* and *her*

Those findings of the differences between adjectives frequently used to modify *man* and *woman* are rather interesting. Let's try to explore this topic even further by comparing the nouns which frequently follow the possessives *his* and *her*. If we found interesting results with how *man* and *woman* are modified by descriptive adjectives, maybe we could also gain some insights about the nouns which follow *his* and *her*. Basically, we're comparing if men and women own and possess different things.

Step 1: In the COCA, click *Compare* and enter *his* and *her* in the search bar

Step 2: Next to Collocates, click noun.ALL in the drop-down menu

Step 3: Set the collocation window at 4L–4R

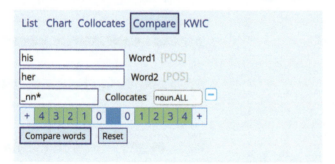

Step 4: Click *Compare words*

WORD 1 (W1): HIS (1.29)

	WORD	W1	W2	W1/W2	SCORE
1	TOUCHDOWN	324	0	648.0	502.2
2	INNINGS	322	0	644.0	499.1
3	HOMER	283	0	566.0	438.7
4	PLAYOFF	236	0	472.0	365.8
5	PITCHING	219	0	438.0	339.5
6	POSTSEASON	204	0	408.0	316.2
7	GOATEE	182	0	364.0	282.1
8	REGIMENT	171	0	342.0	265.1
9	RECEIVERS	167	0	334.0	258.9
10	TOUCHDOWNS	167	0	334.0	258.9
11	BRONCOS	156	0	312.0	241.8
12	PUTT	151	0	302.0	234.1
13	OBAMA	147	0	294.0	227.9
14	CARDINALS	146	0	292.0	226.3
15	HAMSTRING	145	0	290.0	224.8

WORD 2 (W2): HER (0.78)

	WORD	W2	W1	W2/W1	SCORE
1	SARI	188	0	376.0	485.2
2	KNITTING	176	0	352.0	454.2
3	MOTHERHOOD	176	0	352.0	454.2
4	UTERUS	155	0	310.0	400.0
5	FEMININITY	120	0	240.0	309.7
6	FETUS	120	0	240.0	309.7
7	MIDWIFE	120	0	240.0	309.7
8	GIRLHOOD	114	0	228.0	294.2
9	WOMANHOOD	112	0	224.0	289.0
10	OVARIES	111	0	222.0	286.4
11	HUBBY	106	0	212.0	273.5
12	BOOBS	105	0	210.0	271.0
13	WEEPING	105	0	210.0	271.0
14	CONVENT	103	0	206.0	265.8
15	NIGHTDRESS	103	0	206.0	265.8

Notice in the results that the data is now sorted by score/ratio rather than frequency. In contrast to the previous data output in search 3, these words are ranked by their uniqueness rather than their frequency. For example, *touchdown* is not the most frequent noun following *his*, but it is the most likely not to be used with *woman*. Again, it is important to perform focused searches to narrow your findings, but it is equally valuable to understand the data which is produced.

Search 5: Has the way the United States discusses *immigration* and *immigrants* changed?

In recent years, the topic of immigration has been commonly discussed in political debates. It is perhaps possible to think that such attention and focus on immigration and immigrants has been a recent phenomenon; however, that is not true. In the United States, immigration has often appeared in public discussion. It would possibly be revealing then to track how immigration and immigrants have been discussed over time and whether any interesting and insightful trends can be discovered in the data.

Step 1: Navigate to the COHA

corpus.byu.edu
corpora, size, queries = better resources, more insight

Created by Mark Davies, BYU. Overview, search types, looking at variation, corpus-based resources, updates.

The most widely used online corpora -- more than 130,000 distinct researchers, teachers, and students each month.

English	# words	language/dialect	time period	compare
NOW Corpus NEW	2.8 billion+	20 countries / Web	2010-yesterday	
Global Web-Based English (GloWbE)	1.9 billion	20 countries / Web	2012-13	
Wikipedia Corpus	1.9 billion	English	-2014	Info
Hansard Corpus (British Parliament)	1.6 billion	British	1803-2005	Info
Corpus of Contemporary American English (COCA)	520 million	American	1990-2015	★ ★ ★ ★ ★
Corpus of Historical American English (COHA)	400 million	American	1810-2009	★ ★
TIME Magazine Corpus	100 million	American	1923-2006	
Corpus of American Soap Operas	100 million	American	2001-2012	★
British National Corpus (BYU-BNC)*	100 million	British	1980s-1993	★ ★
Strathy Corpus (Canada)	50 million	Canadian	1970s-2000s	
CORE Corpus NEW	50 million	Web registers	-2014	
Other languages				
Corpus del Español (see also...)	100 million	Spanish	1200s-1900s	★
Corpus do Português (see also...)	45 million	Portuguese	1300s-1900s	
N-grams				
Google Books: American English	155 billion	American	1500s-2000s	★
Google Books: British English	34 billion	British	1500s-2000s	
Google Books: One Million Books	89 billion	Am/Br	1500s-2000s	
Google Books: Spanish	45 billion	Spanish	1500s-2000s	

Step 2: Click the *Collocates* search option

Step 3: Enter *immigra** in the search bar

Step 4: Select adj.ALL from the drop-down menu

Step 5: Click *Find collocates*

List Chart Collocates Compare KWIC

immigra*   Word/phrase [POS]

_j*   Collocates adj.ALL (−)

+ 4 3 2 1 0   0 1 2 3 4 +

Find collocates   Reset

Step 6: Analyse results

#		CONTEXT	ALL	1810	1820	1830	1840	1850	1860	1870	1880	1890	1900	1910	1920	1930	1940	1950	1960	1970	1980	1990	2000
1		ILLEGAL	311														3	5	2	8	56	98	139
2		NEW	269			1		3		2	7	10	3	13	19	10	7	13	11	20	38	51	61
3		JEWISH	176									1	8	6	3	31	42	9	3	14	18	23	18
4		OTHER	163			2			4	1	5	9	5	19	8	8	13	15	5	13	22	28	
5		EUROPEAN	143				1	1	3			9	11	7	13	9	6	7	7	14	8	15	16	16
6		RECENT	134			1	2	1	1	1	1	2	8	15	7	3	10	6	6	2	22	21	25
7		IRISH	133					1	3	3	4	4	7	6	5	6	15	9	10	15	9	7	18	11
8		AMERICAN	125						1			1	4	3	10	13	14	8	4	3	9	19	13	23
9		CHINESE	117					2	20	26	5	4	5	1	3	3	1	3	1	2	11	6	28
10		FOREIGN	116	1		1	2	11	7	15	13	14	13	8	10	2	4	3	1	6	1	4	
11		GERMAN	105					2	2	4	8	6	12	2	6	9	6	7	1	7	14	19	
12		ITALIAN	103								1	4	12	7	10	4	6	9	13	9	4	15	9
13		GREAT	87			2		3	2	5	4	9	9	11	4	7		3	9	1	6	6	6
14		LARGE	87					3	1	5	7	11	7	11	5	4	4	1	4	2	6	7	9
15		LEGAL	77												1			1	1		7	40	27

Carefully review the results and record your findings. You could also try explaining your results to a friend or classmate. An important skill to develop for university is the ability to describe graphs and charts and share information in a clear, concise, and comprehensible way to a person who may not know much about the topic. You can use these searches as opportunities to explore language but also as conversation starters to help you practise explaining complex information.

YOUR TURN 4.3

In this search, you compared trends in the use of *immigrant* and *immigration*. Think of another topic such as immigration and explore how the way it has been discussed has changed over time. In your investigation, think carefully about your search, the corpus you should use, and how you can most effectively find the necessary data. Make notes on your findings and share a summary with a friend or classmate.

Findings:

_____

_____

_____

Search 6: *Undocumented immigrant* or *illegal immigrant?*

In a 2007 Public Broadcasting Service (PBS) interview with Maria Hinojosa, Nobel Peace Prize winner Elie Wiesel stated:

> *No human being is illegal. Human beings can be beautiful or more beautiful, they can be right or wrong, but illegal? How can a human being be illegal?*

This statement helped motivate discussions of whether *illegal immigrant* is a problematic expression because of how it presents a human as illegal. Critics of the term *illegal immigrant* have suggested that the term *undocumented immigrant* is more appropriate, and in recent years, some newspapers and organisations have adopted *undocumented* rather than *illegal*. While it seems increasingly common to hear the use *undocumented* in these discussions, does *illegal* still remain the most used term? Let's examine the corpus to see if there have been any changes. Since you used the COHA to look at change over time in the previous search, let's use the Google Ngram Viewer and the NOW Corpus for this search to see recent patterns with the use of these terms.

Step 1: Go to the Google Ngram Viewer

Step 2: Enter *undocumented immigrants* and *illegal immigrants* and click *Search lots of books*

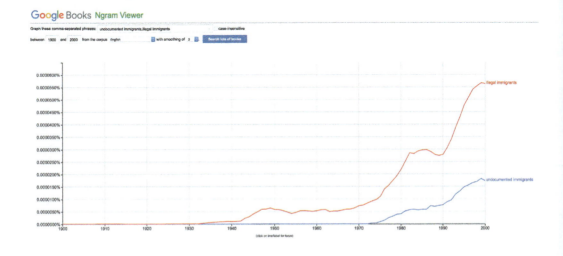

Step 3: Go to https://corpus.byu.edu and enter the News on the Web
         (NOW) Corpus

Step 4: Click the drop-down menu and select adj.ALL

Step 5: Enter *immigra** in the search bar and click *Find matching strings*

List Chart Collocates Compare KWIC

_j* immigra*   adj.ALL   ⊟

Find matching strings   Reset

Step 6: View results

		CONTEXT	FREQ	
1		ILLEGAL IMMIGRANTS	15312	
2		UNDOCUMENTED IMMIGRANTS	6523	
3		ILLEGAL IMMIGRATION	6293	
4		NEW IMMIGRANTS	2617	
5		ILLEGAL IMMIGRANT	2481	
6		FEDERAL IMMIGRATION	2008	
7		MEXICAN IMMIGRANTS	1696	
8		NEW IMMIGRATION	1630	
9		MUSLIM IMMIGRATION	1595	
10		MASS IMMIGRATION	1412	
11		MUSLIM IMMIGRANTS	1361	
12		IRISH IMMIGRANTS	1352	
13		COMPREHENSIVE IMMIGRATION	1316	
14		CANADIAN IMMIGRATION	1137	
15		UNAUTHORIZED IMMIGRANTS	1104	

Step 7: Return to search and click the *Collocates* option, enter *immigra**, and select adj.ALL from the Collocates drop-down menu

List Chart Collocates Compare KWIC

immigra*		Word/phrase	adj.ALL	⊟
_j*		Collocates	adj.ALL	⊟

+ 4 3 2 1 0   0 1 2 3 4 +

Find collocates   Reset

Step 8: View and reflect upon the results

		CONTEXT	FREQ	
1		ILLEGAL	25750	
2		UNDOCUMENTED	8228	
3		NEW	7803	
4		OTHER	4589	
5		MUSLIM	4516	
6		LEGAL	3446	
7		FEDERAL	3278	
8		IRISH	3193	
9		RECENT	2634	
10		MEXICAN	2571	
11		CANADIAN	2371	
12		NATIONAL	2149	
13		AMERICAN	2109	
14		CHINESE	2101	
15		MASS	1821	

These are interesting first steps into further analysis of the language used when discussing immigration in the United States. You may wish to explore further by comparing how *immigrants* and *immigration* are discussed in corpora collected in various English-speaking countries. You could do this by exploring the BNC, the Strathy Corpus of Canadian English, or by searching the GloWbE Corpus of English from 21 English-speaking countries. Investigating whether nations are similar or different in their discussion of this issue may be quite revealing.

Search 7: On fleek? What does that mean?

There's a popular website called Overheard where people post strange or funny things they hear people say in their daily life. As a language learner, you may hear an expression or word that is new to you and whose meaning is not easy to determine from the immediate context. It can be interesting and beneficial to look up the word or phrase in a corpus to see multiple examples. This process can help you understand the meaning of the word or phrase but also help you to see how you can use it in your own communication. Let's search for a recently created word and phrase in the corpus to see what we can discover. The phrase we will look for is *on fleek* and is used with increasing frequency by young people in the United States.

Step 1: Go to the COCA

Step 2: Click the *List* option, enter *on fleek*, and click *Find matching strings*

List	Chart Collocates Compare KWIC

on fleek   [POS]

Find matching strings   Reset

☐ Sections Texts/Virtual Sort/Limit Options

Sorry, there are no matching records. You may wish to do one of the following:

1. Make sure the frequency limits are set correctly (MIN FREQ and checkbox)
2. Select a less restrictive set of sections (genres or time periods)
3. Check the search syntax

Interesting! The phrase is so new in the language that the 560 million word corpus does not have one example of it being used. You'll need to look in a more up-to-date corpus to find samples of the phrase. This is an excellent example of why choosing the correct corpus for your search is so important.

Step 3: Go the NOW Corpus

Step 4: Click the *List* option, enter *on fleek*, and click *Find matching strings*

	■	CONTEXT	FREQ
1	☐	ON FLEEK	340

Step 5: Click *on fleek* and read some of the sample sentences

How is it used in the sample sentences? Does *on fleek* seem to be a positive or negative description? What things does it seem to be describing? Let's search further.

Step 6: Click the *Collocates* search option

Step 7: Keep *on fleek* in the search bar

Step 8: Select noun.ALL from the Collocates drop-down menu

Step 9: Set the collocation window at 4L–4R and click *Find collocates*

```
List  Chart  Collocates  Compare  KWIC

on fleek                Word/phrase [POS]
_nn*           Collocates  noun.ALL   ⊖
 +  4  3  2  1  0     0  1  2  3  4  +
Find collocates    Reset
```

Step 10: View results

		CONTEXT	FREQ
1	☐	EYEBROWS	26
2	☐	BROWS	22
3	☐	MAKEUP	13
4	☐	HAIR	11
5	☐	GAME	9

Perhaps you will never use *on fleek* in your own communication. There may be other unfamiliar idioms that you overhear though that you will wish to use, and corpus study can help you integrate these into your vocabulary. So, the next time you hear a new word or encounter an unfamiliar idiom, search a corpus and see what you discover.

YOUR TURN 4.4

What have you overheard recently? What expression has recently left you confused? If you cannot think of an example to search, you could search for the expression 'the GOAT' that appeared in one of the concordance lines for *on fleek*. What does it mean to call someone or something 'the GOAT'?

_____

_____

_____

Complete a search using the appropriate corpus to investigate your word or phrase. Explain your findings.

_____

_____

_____

Search 8: What do your tweets say about you?

In this age of social media, it is highly probable that you have accounts across several social media platforms. You may post pictures to Instagram, post messages on Facebook, or follow your favourite celebrities on Twitter. Considering how popular these platforms are, it will be interesting to analyse what our and others' social media communications may reveal about us. One site that allows you to analyse a person's tweets is called AnalyzeWords. Open the site and let's see what we can discover.

Step 1: Go to http://www.analyzewords.com/

ANALYZE WORDS

What does AnalyzeWords do?
AnalyzeWords helps reveal your personality by looking at how you use words. It is based on good scientific research connecting word use to who people are. So go to town - enter your Twitter name or the handles of friends, lovers, or Hollywood celebrities to learn about their emotions, social styles, and the ways they think.

Twitter Handle: @ [   ] | Analyze Tweets | The Development Team
The Science Behind AnalyzeWords

Step 2: Enter the Twitter handle of one of your favourite musicians or actresses

Tip: If you don't use Twitter, some of the most popular accounts are Katy Perry (@katyperry), Justin Bieber (@justinbieber), and Taylor Swift (@taylorswift13).

Twitter Handle: @ justinbieber | **Analyze Tweets** |

Step 3: Click *Analyze Tweets*

Tip: If you scroll over the category titles, it will explain how the analysis is conducted.

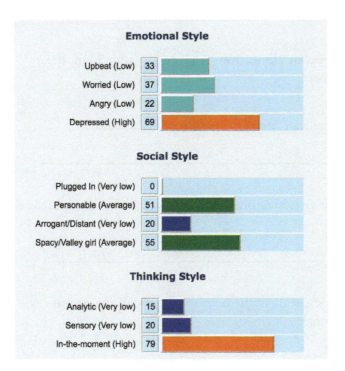

What does the celebrity's tweets say about him or her? What type of words do you think are used to create the ratings for upbeat, worried, personable, and the other categories? These searches using AnalyzeWords can lead to fun and engaging conversation in classrooms and help students to think more critically about language use.

YOUR TURN 4.5

Analyse your own tweets or those from a favourite athlete, musician, politician, or organisation.

1. What do the results indicate about the person or organisation?

   _____

2. Why do you think the person or organisation scored high in some areas but low in others?

   _____

3. What can the results show about the possible purpose of the person's or the organisation's profile?

   _____

5 BUILDING YOUR OWN CORPUS

TO THIS POINT, we have only completed searches in publicly available, free online corpora and corpus tools. These are great resources and enable a wide variety of searches, but there may be a time when you have the need to build your own corpus to answer particular questions. For example, you may wish to analyse expert writing in your field of study and compare characteristics from expert writing with your own work. Or perhaps you want to study language use in political speeches, fan fiction, business writing, or opinion-editorials from your local newspaper. There are many tools and resources available to help you do this.

In the following activity, we will see how to compile and analyse your own specialised corpus designed to meet your own needs and objectives. For this illustration, imagine you are interested in studying expert-level business writing. After much consideration of which type of text you should and could collect, you decide to compile letters to the shareholders written by Fortune 500 companies in the United States in hopes that studying these polished letters will help you learn about and improve your own business writing. For this tutorial, you may download several shareholder letters or use texts you already have saved on your computer.

Step 1: Create a folder on your desktop or hard drive where you can save your files

This is important because some corpus tools will not read and process files that are stored in a cloud system. For example, if you save your files in a cloud service such as Dropbox, the corpus tool AntConc will sometimes not be able to process your texts.

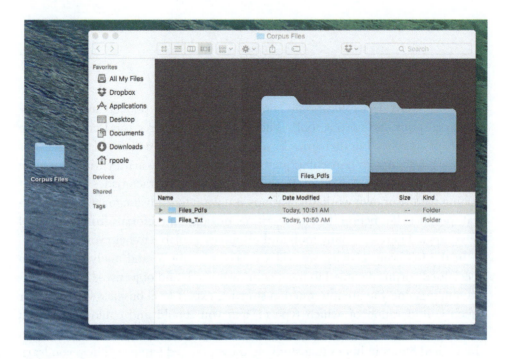

Step 2: Collect the files which you wish to analyse

Remember that your collection should be organised to answer a particular question or help you explore a special interest. It is probably wise to set some criteria that you can follow when choosing texts to include in your corpus. For example, you may want to study authors of a particular time period, abstracts from a specific academic journal, articles from a local newspaper, and so on. In this example, the criterion for selection is letters to the shareholders from the top Fortune 500 companies in 2016.

Step 3: Save/convert your files to .txt files

If the files you want to collect and analyse are saved as .doc or .docx, the process is rather simple. You only need to open the file, click *Save as*, and select .txt from the file format menu. However, if the files you collected are pdfs, you will need to try one of the following solutions: (1) You can copy and paste the text from the pdf into a txt file. This process can sometimes produce some strange symbols in the text, so you will need to 'clean up' your text before you load it into the corpus tool. (2) If you have a large pdf file, you can use a service like ABBYY Online to convert your pdf into text. The site will allow you to do 10 pages for free, but it will charge you a small amount for additional text.

To Our Shareholders

ExxonMobil is dedicated to generating long-term value for you, our shareholders. We strive to remain the industry leader in safely supplying the energy necessary to support economies and improve the lives of billions of people, while at the same time protecting the environment. This challenge is what drives the thousands of men and women of ExxonMobil to push the frontiers of science and technology, develop new products and resources, optimize our operations, and continually improve.

As you will read, we achieve success through discipline in our capital spending, advantaged project execution, operational excellence, and a relentless focus on business fundamentals. With our strong balance sheet, prudent management, and deep inventory of opportunities, ExxonMobil is uniquely positioned to create value through the commodity price cycle.

Step 4: Clean your txt files

Check your newly created txt file to ensure it is 'clean'. Sometimes when you copy text from a pdf into a txt file, odd characters will appear in the text. For example, when the text in the 'To our shareholders' pdf was copied into TextEdit, each instance of *ie* was change to %. There are several reasons why this occurs, but fortunately, it is rather easy to correct.

To Our Shareholders

ExxonMobil is dedicated to generating long-term value for you, our shareholders. We strive to remain the industry leader %in safely supplying the energy necessary to support econom%s and improve the lives of billions of people, while at the same time protecting the environment. This challenge is what drives the thousands of men and women of ExxonMobil to push the front %rs of sc%nce and technology, develop new products and resources, optimize our operations, and continually improve.

As you will read, we ach%ve success through discipline in our capital spending, advantaged project execution, operational excellence, and a relentless focus on business fundamentals. With our strong balance sheet, prudent management, and deep inventory of opportunit%s, ExxonMobil is uniquely positioned to create value through the commodity price cycle.

By selecting *Edit* → *Find* → *Find and replace* in TextEdit, you can quickly clean the document.

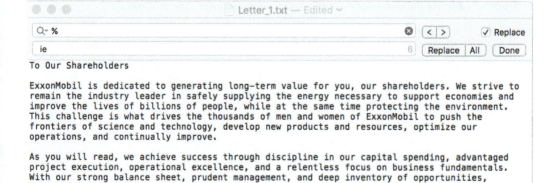

Step 5: Build the corpus

Continue to collect documents and create txt files until you feel you have an adequate number of files to represent the genre which you selected for study.

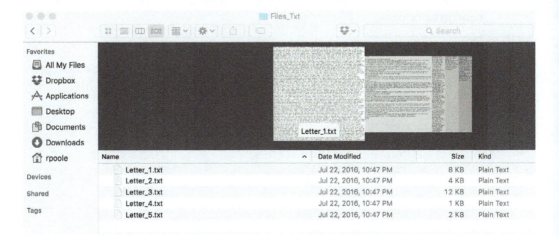

Step 6: Download the appropriate Windows or Mac version of AntConc at http://www.laurenceanthony.net/software/antconc/

AntConc is a free and user-friendly corpus tool that can perform a variety of functions such as creating word lists, searching collocates, and generating concordance lines.

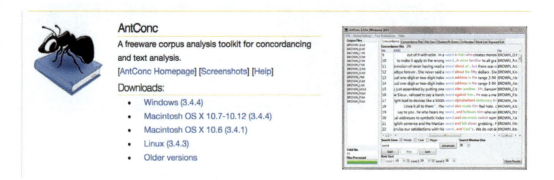

Step 7: Open AntConc

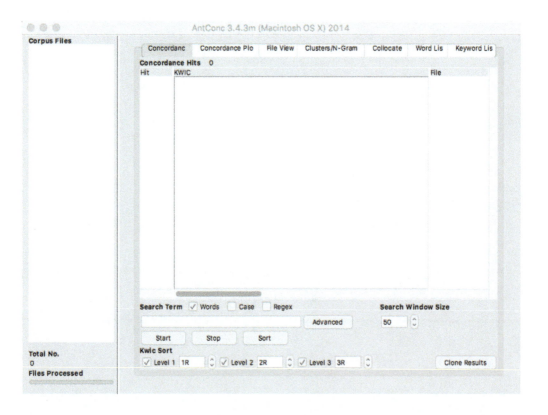

Step 8: Open your saved txt files

To open files, click *File*, *Open Files*, and select your files from your desktop folder.

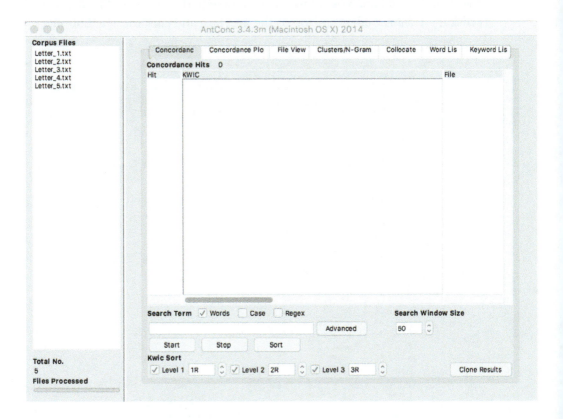

Step 9: Create a word list

In AntConc, it is necessary to create the word list before you can complete any other searches and analysis. Thus, the first thing to do once your files are loaded is click the *Word List* tab at the top of the interface and click the *Start* button.

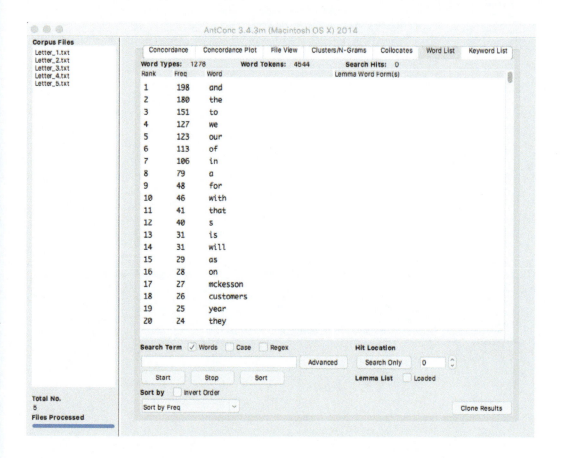

Step 10: Analyse your corpus

Across the top of the AntConc interface are a variety of search functions for investigating your texts. Perhaps the most frequently used option allows you to view concordance lines of a word of interest from your word list. There are two ways to view concordance lines: (1) Click on the word in the *Word List*. (2) Click on the *Concordance* tab at the top left of the interface, enter in the search bar the word which you would like to analyse, and click the *Start* button. Both of these techniques will allow you to view all of the sentences that use the word in which you are interested.

The other functions of AntConc are:

- *Concordance Plot*: This function allows you to view where in the text the word appears. This may be useful if you are studying expert writing in your field, as it will allow you to, for example, see where certain transition words are used in academic writing.
- *File View*: This function allows you to view the broader context in which a word is used.
- *Clusters/N-Grams*: A cluster or n-gram is group of words which appear frequently in your corpus. For example, some of the most common 3-word n-grams in the letters are *place to work, a better place, across the company, around the world*, and *as well as*. If you are working to improve your fluency, many believe it can be more beneficial to study frequent n-grams rather than frequent words.
- *Collocates*: As seen in the other corpora we have investigated, this option allows you to see which words frequently are used together with your search term.
- *Keyword List*: The keyword list function is powerful and insightful, but it takes more time to perform. When generated, this list shows the words which are statistically key within your corpus. When working with corpora, a general word list will always have articles (*a, an, the*), conjunctions (*and, but, so*), and prepositions (*to, in, of*) at the top of your list. However, since these words are at the top of nearly every word list, perhaps they do not help us see and understand what is unique about the corpus we are studying. When creating a keyword list, AntConc compares the text files you wish to analyse (often referred to as the node corpus) with a much larger corpus called a reference corpus. When AntConc compares the two corpora, it removes the words which appear frequently in both corpora and creates a list of words that appear frequently only in the node corpus. Thus, these words are called keywords because they are particularly important and unique to the texts

that you are analysing. However, to complete this search function, you must have a large reference corpus. For instance, to create a list of keywords for the 5 letters to the shareholders, we would need a reference corpus that contains at least 5 times as many words as our node corpus. Further, we need the reference corpus to also be business writing. In another example, we could do a keyword analysis of several of our own essays in comparison with a larger corpus of essays from other writers. As stated, this can be a tremendously insightful process, but it does take more time to perform.

NOTE FOR TEACHERS

THIS TYPE OF do-it-yourself (DIY) corpus project could be implemented in a variety of classes. Students could collect letters to the editor from a local newspaper, abstracts from a journal in their field of study, or articles on an issue of local interest such as the construction of a new pipeline. In a composition class, students could collect articles written from different perspectives on a controversial issue and write an essay describing and explaining the variation. Such a project gives learners an opportunity to develop important analytic abilities as they collect, analyse, and then write about language in use.

In addition to student-centred DIY projects, teachers can create their own learner corpus from student essays. A corpus of student essays can be used for a variety of in-class activities. For example, an instructor could extract all instances of the linking adverbial *however* from their student essay corpus. Students could discuss whether the adverbial is used effectively and whether it is punctuated correctly.

These are only a few of the many possibilities of how instructors can implement language-focused, student-centred corpus activities in the classroom.

YOUR TURN 5.1

In the illustrations throughout this chapter, the corpus used to demonstrate the steps was a compilation of letters to the shareholders of US-based Fortune 500 companies. These letters were collected to make possible an investigation of business writing. Through an analysis of the letters, it is possible to see which adjectives and adverbs are used frequently, how people are referred to in business writing, and what types of modals are commonly used. This corpus was built to be analysed by language learners in an English class for learners who desire to study for a degree in business. Answer the following questions.

1. What type of corpus you would like to build?

_____

_____

2. What texts would you collect?

_____

_____

3. Where would you find the texts?

_____

_____

4. What would you explore in your analysis?

_____

_____

5. How could the information you find in your analysis be beneficial to you?

_____

_____

CORPUS RESOURCES

ALL OF THE corpora and corpus tools listed below are free and available online at the web addresses provided. While all of the resources listed can be used for language learning, the resources marked with an asterisk (*) are specifically designed and created for language learners.

AntConc	A corpus analysis tool for building and analysing corpora	http://www.laurenceanthony.net/software/antconc/
British Academic Spoken English Corpus (BASE)	Approximately 1.2 million words of spoken British academic English	https://the.sketch engine.co.uk/open/
British Academic Written English Corpus (BAWE)	Approximately 7 million words of written British academic English	https://the.sketch engine.co.uk/open/
British National Corpus (BNC)	100 million words of written and spoken British English from the late twentieth century until 1993	https://corpus.byu.edu
Business Letter Corpus	Approximately 1 million words from US and UK business letter samples	http://www.someya-net.com/concordancer/
Corpus of Contemporary American English (COCA)	Over 560 million words of American English from 1990–2015 collected from across a variety of registers	https://corpus.byu.edu

Corpus of Historical American English (COHA)	400 million words of American English from 1810–2009	https://corpus.byu.edu
*FLAX Interactive Language Learning	A collection of learner-focused tools, user-friendly search interface, no registration required	http://flax.nzdl.org/greenstone3/flax
Global Web-Based English Corpus (GloWbE)	Approximately 2 billion words of English collected from 20 countries	https://corpus.byu.edu
Google Ngram Viewer	A massive, billion word web corpus, no registration required	https://books.google.com/ngrams
Hong Kong Corpus of Spoken English	Approximately 1 million words from various technical and professional contexts	http://rcpce.engl.polyu.edu.hk/index.html
*LexTutor	Website with a variety of corpus-based activities for language learners	http://www.lextutor.ca/
Michigan Corpus of Academic Spoken English (MICASE)	Approximately 1.8 million words of spoken academic English	http://quod.lib.umich.edu/m/micase/
Michigan Corpus of Upper-Level Student Papers (MICUSP)	A corpus of students papers collected across 16 academic disciplines, no registration required	http://micusp.elicorpora.info/
News on the Web Corpus (NOW)	4.65 billion words from 20 countries updated daily from internet language use	https://corpus.byu.edu
*Sketch Engine for Language Learning (SkELL)	More than 1 billion words from a variety of sources, user-friendly interface, no registration required	http://skell.sketchengine.co.uk/run.cgi/skell
State of the Union Corpus	A corpus of all US presidential State of the Union addresses from 1790–2017	http://stateoftheunion.onetwothree.net/index.shtml

Strathy Corpus of Canadian English	50 million words from a range of texts	https://corpus.byu.edu
Time Magazine Corpus	100 million words from the American periodical from 1923–2006	https://corpus.byu.edu
WebCorp Live	Real-time concordance of web language	http://www.webcorp.org.uk/live/index.jsp
Wikipedia Corpus	A massive corpus of approximately 2 billion words from more than 4 million Wikipedia articles	https://corpus.byu.edu
wordandphrase.info	A corpus resource, no registration required	https://www.wordandphrase.info

FURTHER READING

THE FOLLOWING TEXTS will be useful to graduate students and language instructors who wish to further explore corpus linguistics and its application in language learning classrooms.

Bennett, G. (2010), *Using Corpora in the Language Learning Classroom: Corpus Linguistics for Teachers*, Ann Arbor, MI: University of Michigan Press.

Liu, D. and L. Lei (2017), *Using Corpora for Language Learning and Teaching*, Alexandria, VA: TESOL Press.

O'Keeffe, A., M. McCarthy and R. Carter (2007), *From Corpus to Classroom: Language Use and Language Teaching*, Cambridge: Cambridge University Press.

Reppen, R. (2010), *Using Corpora in the Language Classroom*, Cambridge: Cambridge University Press.

Timmis, I. (2015), *Corpus Linguistics for ELT*, New York: Routledge.

GLOSSARY

booster: A booster is word such as *always* or *absolutely* which increases the strength of an assertion or claim.

collocate: A collocate is word which appears frequently with another word.

collocation window: In a collocate search, the default collocation window is often 4L–4R. The search produces results that show the words 4 to the left and 4 to the right of the search word. The window can be modified to narrow search results.

concordance lines: Concordance lines are a type of output display that show all sentences in which a search word appears.

corpus (plural: **corpora**): A corpus is a large, searchable collection of authentic language compiled to represent a particular genre, register, or area of discourse.

corpus linguistics: Corpus linguistics is an approach to language analysis which employs the use of corpora for the study of language.

frequency: The frequency is the total number of times a word occurs in a corpus.

hedge: A hedge such as *might, may*, or *likely* reduces the strength of an assertion or claim.

keyword: In a *KWIC* search, the keyword is the search word and is colour coded according to part of speech. A keyword is also a word which appears at a significantly different frequency in one corpus when compared with a larger reference corpus.

lemma: A lemma is the base word to which a family of words are related. For example, talks, talked, and talking are related to the lemma TALK.

linking adverbial: A linking adverbial, sometimes referred to as a conjunctive adverb or transition word, is a word such as *therefore, however, moreover, additionally*, and others that connect grammatical elements of a sentence. It often begins a sentence and is followed by a comma. It is also used to combine two independent clauses.

per million rate: A per million rate is the number of times a word appears per million words of running language in a corpus. The per million rate is used to compare the frequency of a word in corpora of different sizes. In many corpora, this is often abbreviated to PM or per mil.

register: A register is a variety of language that is used in a particular context for a particular purpose. For example, the variety of formal language used in university classrooms and textbooks can be called an academic register.

INDEX